DAYS OF HEAVEN

DAYS OF HEAVEN

Italia 90 and the Charlton Years

DECLAN LYNCH ～

Gill & Macmillan

For Caroline

Gill & Macmillan Ltd
Hume Avenue, Park West, Dublin 12
with associated companies throughout the world
www.gillmacmillan.ie

© Declan Lynch 2010
978 07171 4637 6

Typography design by Make Communication
Print origination by Carole Lynch
Printed by ColourBooks Ltd, Dublin

This book is typeset in Linotype Minion 12.5/17pt
and Neue Helvetica.

The paper used in this book comes from the wood pulp
of managed forests. For every tree felled, at least one tree
is planted, thereby renewing natural resources.

A CIP catalogue record for this book is available
from the British Library.

5 4 3 2 1

CONTENTS

ACKNOWLEDGMENTS

Special thanks to my friends Dion Fanning, Liam Mackey, Paul Howard, Arthur Mathews, John Waters, Philip Chevron and George Byrne for the excellence of their memories and the blinding clarity of their insights.

Books by Paul Rowan (*The Team That Jack Built*), Derek O'Kelly and Shay Blair *(What's The Story?)*, Andy Townsend and Paul Kimmage (*Andy's Game*) and Roddy Doyle (*The Snapper* and *The Van*) and Dermot Bolger's play *In High Germany* also brought me back.

Remembering Bill Graham and Dermot Morgan and Frank Lynch.

| INTRODUCTION

When it was suggested to me that I write about my recollections of the Charlton years, on the occasion of the 20th anniversary of Italia 90, my thoughts naturally turned to a scene in a toilet in New York City.

It was a Sunday afternoon in June 1988 and the toilet was in a bar on 7th Avenue called Mulligan's, which, by an extraordinarily happy accident, was also the name of the pub on Poolbeg Street in Dublin where I was doing much of my drinking back home — oh, how I laughed as I supped another glass of Schlitz and marvelled at a world which could contain such coincidences.

But then it had been a weekend of marvels.

I had been sent to New York to do a feature on Christy Moore for the *Sunday Independent,* for whom I had just started to write, mainly about Irish show-business personalities — the first was Hal Roach, then there was Sonny Knowles, so it must have seemed logical at the time to move on to Christy Moore. A lot of things seemed logical then, which do not necessarily seem logical now.

And this would not be the usual 800-word profile. It would be a special four-page glossy pull-out, illustrated with pictures of Christy stretching back to his childhood, to mark not just the life and times of the greatest living Irishman, but the fact that he was in New York to play the Carnegie Hall.

This was big stuff. Big enough for me to be accompanied by one Donal Doherty, an *Independent* photographer of renown, the sort of crack lensman you can still see on RTÉ's *Reeling In The Years,* taking pictures of Charlie Haughey in the throes of some nightmarish

Fianna Fáil heave. A man who had been a witness to various national traumas, which perhaps helps to explain why he was happy to be in New York on this particular weekend.

Because back in the old world, on the day after Christy played Carnegie Hall, the Republic of Ireland would be playing England in Stuttgart in the first game of Euro 88. Which was big stuff, too. And which will eventually bring us back to that scene in the toilet of Mulligan's of 7th Avenue.

But first I should mention that we flew to New York via Heathrow, where we saw George Best. He was catching a flight to America, too. Perhaps it was just coincidence that the most gifted player ever to come from our island needed to be on another continent, perhaps even another planet, on the weekend that the Boys In Green were stepping on to football's main stage. But at that moment I thought, it must be a great life George has, heading off to California unencumbered, whenever he feels like it, while the likes of me and the crack lensman are lugging our kit through the airport, the fear rising within us that we are going to miss our flight and miss all that big stuff. Airport security made Doherty empty out every roll of film he had in his large box of photographic tricks while the plane was revving up and seemingly certain to go without us. Ireland, lest we forget, was a world leader in terrorism at that time.

Even though it was general knowledge that he was an alcoholic, I did not know enough about alcoholism then to come to the more likely conclusion, that George was probably not sauntering off to some rendezvous on the West Coast without a care in the world, but was almost certainly boarding a flight for god-knows-where, with about ten dollars in his pocket and nothing else left in the world except the clothes that he wore and the inescapable fact that he was still George Best. Nor did I understand at any meaningful level that the Republic's best-loved footballer, on whom we would perhaps be depending most in Stuttgart, the great Paul McGrath, was himself very far gone down that line. In fact, I did not even know enough about alcoholism then to know that I was getting a touch of it myself.

But I thought I knew about it. I was planning to raise the issue with Christy Moore when I sat down with him in some hotel room in New York — if we ever got there, which, as the Heathrow security men emptied the 54th tube of Donal's film out onto the counter, seemed unlikely.

Christy at the time was one of the few famous Irishmen who had spoken openly about his tragic love affair with the bottle, and indeed had written a song about it, 'Delirium Tremens'.

Yes, I would be asking him about that.

Not that this flood of recollections will be all about drink, by any means. But I sense that most readers, being honest, would have to agree that it must be at least *partly* about drink. That when they look back on those days, on Euro 88 and Italia 90 and the rest of what we call the Charlton era, it certainly wasn't all about football. It was an overwhelming combination of so many things, a journey the like of which we had never made before, and all we know for sure, is that very few of us made it entirely sober.

But we got to New York anyway, the photographer and I.

We got to the Sheraton Hotel on the Friday night and soon I was in Mulligan's bar on 7th Avenue, having a beer and watching a baseball game on the TV. And then the lads from the Gate Theatre arrived in.

In what now seems like some sort of a montage of the emerging Irish nation, the Gate Theatre was on Broadway with its production of *Juno and the Paycock*, directed by Joe Dowling, starring Donal McCann and John Kavanagh, on the weekend that Christy Moore would play Carnegie Hall and the Republic would play England in Stuttgart.

Interestingly, though we had been living through a troubled time in Ireland, we were still capable of sending high-class stuff to America, despite it all, perhaps because of it all. *Juno* was great, but no doubt it was happening at least partly because of its continuing relevance to 'the situation', the fact that there was still an IRA, capable of an atrocity such as the Enniskillen bombing, little more than six months before.

I think it was the actor Donagh Deeney, who was playing The Furniture Removal Man in *Juno*, who brought me into the company that night in Mulligan's bar. Maybe it just happened by that ancient process of recognition that always draws Paddy to Paddy, on foreign soil.

I can't remember if Joe Savino was there. Joe was playing Johnny Boyle in *Juno*. From the days when he sang in a rock 'n' roll band, I had run into Joe on many occasions in my life, almost always in bars, and almost always when, by some unhappy accident, I had been drinking more than he. Over the years, I must have talked more shit to Joe than to most people. Which means that a fog of guilt and denial descends upon me whenever I think of him.

But if he wasn't there, he should have been.

We were all so excited about everything. We were so excited to be in New York; we were particularly excited to be in a bar in New York with so much to look forward to, be it Christy at the Carnegie Hall or *Juno*, which was starting its previews the following Wednesday in the John Golden Theatre, or Ireland playing England.

Not that we were looking forward to Ireland playing England in the same way that we were looking forward to the other stuff.

Because, as well as excitement, there was also a deep fear in our hearts, as we faced into that battle. A fear that Jack's team might be no good, after all, and that they would get beaten by England, not just 2-0 or something vaguely respectable, but beaten badly. Beaten out the door.

As we proceed with this thing, we will examine this fatalistic streak in the Irish character, and how the events of the Charlton years challenged us to look at ourselves anew in this regard. To see ourselves as people who did not always need to be afraid of making eejits out of ourselves in the international arena.

But on this Friday night in Mulligan's of New York, we were still on the cusp of all that. We were somewhat astonished to be at Euro 88 at all, but we still harboured that fear that on Sunday we would be found out, in the most disgraceful way.

Yes, these men who were talented enough and ambitious enough and self-confident enough to be standing on the Broadway stage alongside your Donal McCanns and your John Kavanaghs and your Maureen Potters, essaying the work of O'Casey in front of the most brutal critics of the New York theatre, were not immune to these old, old fears.

Elsewhere in the city, during that Broadway run, my friend Philip Chevron of the Radiators and The Pogues would be having a night off from Poguetry in order to give the town a new lick of paint with said Maureen Potter. And he believes that fellow Pogue, Terry Woods headed off into the Manhattan night with his buddy Donal McCann. Chevron also believes he drank with the actor Mick Egan, who played the Sewing Machine Vendor, in *Juno*. And Shane MacGowan was out there too, doing what Shane does, in New York.

And all of these Irishmen and women, even the most illustrious of them, at the peak of their powers, would have had their moments when they feared chaos on an unprecedented scale in Stuttgart. Chaos, and ultimately catastrophe, for the Republic.

There was also the lesser fear that most of us here in New York on this weekend wouldn't actually see the match. Many of us, in fact, were secretly relieved that we wouldn't see it, that we would be spared the truth being shoved in our faces.

It must be remembered that even in America back then, there were few big screens in bars, and even fewer showing 'soccer' matches. There was also the time difference which meant that even if the company at the Gate could commandeer some bar in Queens or wherever, the match would be happening on Sunday morning, New York time, which effectively ruled out myself and the photographer, who were due to fly back on the Sunday afternoon. And even if we somehow found a bar with a TV showing soccer on ESPN and a very fast car, we were haunted by the certainty that the snapper's suitcase would be emptied out and inspected for about two hours on the way back.

And that would be too much — that, on top of some terrible slaughter.

———

But the Furniture Removal Man and the other guys in Mulligan's were quietly confident that they would actually see the match — Donal McCann had sussed out a place, apparently. Or not, as the case may be.

That's Donal, who joins Christy, Bestie, McGrath, Chevron and arguably Charles Haughey as the sixth alcoholic, not including the author, to appear so far in this narrative.

And Shane MacGowan is in a category of his own.

Though of course, these men had many other strings to their bows.

———

Christy was generous with his time the next day, his driver taking us to various New York settings like Washington Square Park, so that Doherty could take his pictures. Looking ten years younger than he had looked ten years previously, Christy talked about how he had given up the drink and taken up a macrobiotic diet. He had loved butter almost as fiercely as he had loved porter. Now he had become just as fond of carrot juice. Which perhaps accounted for his calmness on this day when he would be playing Carnegie Hall.

He would also speak of his ultimate disillusion with the republican movement after Enniskillen. Which was about time for him, though he got there in the end.

Christy was interested in a book I was reading about Henry Ford, the supreme achiever of the Irish diaspora. We were all interested in the photographer's epic endeavour to buy one of those new car-phone things at the right price from a shop run by a bunch of Latinos, a car-phone thing in New York being fantastically cheaper than a car-phone thing in Ireland.

'My girlfriend comes from Ireland,' the shop owner lied, thinking this might tip the balance his way at a crucial stage of the negotiations, which would ultimately prove fruitless. 'She is from County Bray.'

Christy's was a tight operation, essentially himself, his deeply intelligent manager, former showband singer Mattie Fox, and a sound man. It seemed only right that *Time* magazine carried a small feature about him on the occasion of his visit to America, placing Christy in an international context of timeless roots music. We had come to expect nothing less from an Irish artist of this stature — by now U2 had already sold about ten million copies of *The Joshua Tree*, the Pogues had produced 'Fairytale of New York', the film *My Left Foot* was about to win two Oscars, and Sinead O'Connor was at that stage when, as they say, she could be anything.

But still we could hardly face Ireland v England in Stuttgart without a recurring sense of dread throbbing away in our guts. Ah, there is a deep restlessness in the soul of Paddy, and sure enough it could be seen and heard in snatches in the vicinity of Carnegie Hall that evening.

And let me clarify at the outset that when I refer to Paddy, I am not necessarily excluding myself. Like Afro-Americans with the n-word, I feel it is all right for Paddy to speak of Paddy, because he is himself Paddy, so he is speaking with love and understanding.

There were some Americans in the hall that night — the serious musicologist types who had been reading *Time* magazine — but this was a night for Paddy to be among his own kind and to let himself go. So many of the voices were clearly and ostentatiously from the counties of Ireland that it made a visit to the Gents sound weirdly like some flashback to the dancehall days when the lads would be supping from naggins of whiskey before heading back to the hall to take on the women. Rowdy lads would be reminded by more sensible lads that they needed to behave themselves, to remember that they weren't at home any more.

This form of peer pressure was one which we were starting to see being enforced across the continent of Europe, too, Paddy on Paddy. In the era of football hooliganism, reporters covering Euro 88 would marvel at the way that the Irish would police themselves, how an errant fan with maybe a few beers on him, trying to steal a chocolate muffin from a display counter, would be chastised by his buddies, all quipping good-naturedly.

Back in the grand environs of Carnegie Hall, you could sense there would be no trouble either from Paddy, even from the most vulnerable of us, the alcoholics who would be out in force tonight, hailing Christy the lost leader.

This new wave of self-policing, even of personal responsibility, might have been partly due to the ever-present danger of attracting too much attention to yourself, as an undocumented alien. But there seemed to be a co-ordinated effort on the part of all Paddies everywhere to behave ourselves, now that we were going places. And more importantly, to be seen to be behaving ourselves. And even more importantly, for Paddy to be seen to be behaving himself better than John Bull.

Yes, we were going places — tonight we would celebrate our

national bard at the most storied Hall in the most cultured city on earth, tomorrow we would also celebrate, win, lose or draw.

Except we knew that we wouldn't win.

And we knew that we wouldn't draw.

And we would have to deal with that, in the only way we knew how.

Did I feel any guilt, that I would not be witnessing this defining event in our island story? Not even a twinge, to tell you the truth. In the matter of the Republic of Ireland and of football in Ireland in general, I had paid my dues. My father Frank, who had been involved in football in Athlone all his life, was taking me to see the Republic playing in Dalymount when it would not be unusual to see Eamon Dunphy out there on the park.

But I don't propose to list my full football credentials here — suffice to say that on this day, I felt a bit like the wise peasant who plants the seed, unconcerned that he may not see the harvest. 'My work is done', I thought, as I dropped into Mulligan's on the Sunday for a few more beers for the road.

I even felt some vague disdain for the hordes beyond in Ireland and in Germany, wondering where they had been on a night a long time ago, in 1981, when a few of us from the *Hot Press* magazine had to persuade the barman in a Mount Street pub to get the telly going in a quiet corner of the lounge so that we could watch Belgium beating us 1-0 in the pouring rain, the thunder and lightning in Brussels, denying us qualification for the 1982 World Cup with a late, horribly illegal goal.

It was such nights which had convinced Paddy that success was not for him. That there was nothing inappropriate or unreasonable in his mounting dread of what might be happening in Stuttgart ... what might already have happened in Stuttgart.

Yes, it would be over now, I thought, as I had another one for the road. In a world which had yet to discover the need for everyone to be constantly informed about everything as soon as it happens, in a country which regarded soccer as a girl's game, in a time before texting, you just resigned yourself to finding out about things as best you could — especially if part of you didn't want to find out.

———

So it was that I went to the toilet in Mulligan's bar, where I encountered the actor Joe Savino — Johnny Boyle in *Juno*. It felt surreal then, and it still has shades of the *Twilight Zone*, because normally I would be running into Joe in Larry Tobin's of Duke Street. Suddenly, it seemed that the world was no longer such a big place, for Paddy.

— The score?

— England won.

— Oh fuck.

— They won 7-2.

I believed him, of course.

No Irishman would have disbelieved him, at that time.

— They won 7-2.

— Of course they did.

At some stage Joe took pity on me. As a football man, with a natural inclination towards the truth, he could not let such a lie stand. Ireland had won 1-0.

Ireland had not lost to England, or drawn with England.

Ireland had scored one goal and England had scored no goals, and the match was over now, so Ireland had won.

There was no other way of looking at it.

And they couldn't take it away from us now.

Ireland … had … won.

———

In the hotel lobby that morning, a bunch of Scandinavian pilots and air hostesses had arrived, and I had observed them as Paddy had always observed such people, as a kind of a different species, one to which he could never belong, into whose company he could never be admitted as an equal, his best hope being to entertain them with his antics. I now knew that I was as good as any of them, that Paddy could even win football matches now.

I would be going back to a land transformed. I would be bringing home this tiny T-shirt, with the Manhattan skyline on it.

My daughter, Roseanne, was a month old.

Chapter 1 ～

|TEENAGE KICKS

Y ou should never trust a man who supports the Republic of
Ireland. By this I mean a man who supports the Republic to
the exclusion of all other football teams. It is perfectly normal
and good to support the Republic along with the club you support
for most of the year, be it a League of Ireland club or a Premiership
club, or ideally both — genuine football men have always found it
natural to maintain such a portfolio, and deeply unnatural to pursue
a more narrow, nationalistic line.

At one level, it is simply a matter of putting in the hours. The
genuine football man does it every day of the week, most weeks of
the year, and weekends too. It is a full-time occupation, which gives
him certain rights — the right to comment, for example, on the
game with a certain degree of credibility.

The man who comes across like a football man but who only
supports the Republic is essentially a bullshitter. He may vouch for
his commitment by pointing out that he follows the lads to foreign
countries, but that can also be classed as a drinking holiday, an extension of adolescence into infinity, not the job of work that it should
be. And in a good year, he can get away with about eight matches,
which would hardly represent a month's endeavour for the real
people. He is, in every sense, only here for the beer.

Yet it is his voice, and the voices of many more like him, which have
tended to prevail in our official version of the Charlton years — the
Olé Olé voice, as we know it. It behoves us to question all the received

wisdom on this, even the parts that seem most persuasive, such as the assertion that the unprecedented achievements of Charlton's teams in qualifying for major tournaments gave the Irish a new sort of positive attitude which contributed to the subsequent economic boom.

Personally I would have subscribed to that one, up to a point, and in a lazy-minded way, until I heard it said for about the fourteenth time on RTÉ's *Questions and Answers*, which renders it automatically suspect.

Indeed to gauge the mentality of the Olé Olé crowd, you might recall the way that assembled members of the Irish establishment on *Q&A* would respond to any question about sport, usually the last question, the 'funny' one. They would immediately lapse into a fit of girlish giggling at the 'light relief' provided by the mention of sport, after all their grave reflections on supposedly more serious matters such as, say, the new Fine Gael policy document on neutrality.

These people know nothing. But worse, they do not even know that they know nothing.

So when I hear the consensus forming that the Celtic Tiger can be traced back to the Boys In Green, as they call them, something bothers me. Perhaps they are just reaching for the familiar embrace of a cliché, in this case the one that 'success breeds success'. But if that is the case, what bred the success that Jack had? Is it not also true to say that failure breeds success, inspiring us to do better, to rise above the morass in which we find ourselves? In fact, given the economic and social context in which U2 and the Gate Theatre and Christy Moore were formed, and considering how well they were doing back in the late 1980s, can it not be argued that failure actually breeds success better than success does? It is such a fine line and we need to remind ourselves that the first phase of the Charlton years had ended in failure, or so everyone thought at the time.

It had been universally accepted that Ireland would not qualify for Euro 88, that they would finish second in the Group. Jack's first

campaign had had its uplifting moments — the best research suggests that Olé Olé was first heard in Lansdowne Road around this
time — but with the last match about to be played, in which we
needed Bulgaria to get beaten at home by Scotland, it was clear that
ultimately Jack had failed.

Not that we were too disappointed, this time. We had not actually
been overtly cheated on this occasion and we had not disgraced ourselves. We did not have to look at Eoin Hand and the other lads on the
bench in the pouring rain with their heads in their hands, mourning
another night of appalling misery. We had had our low moments, in
particular a scoreless draw against Scotland at Lansdowne which
would be regarded as one of the most boring football matches ever
played by trained professionals — then again, there was a night in
Hampden Park when we beat the Scots 1-0, which gave us a brief
foretaste of the fine madness which was to come.

Though we had again resigned ourselves to not qualifying, we
would live off these advances, until the next time.

Even the two draws with Belgium had not been without honour
— and in particular the 2-2 result in the Heysel Stadium was viewed
as a moral victory. Which might not seem like progress, for a
country such as ours, where we had so many moral victories, we had
become connoisseurs of the things, noting their unique character-
istics and subtleties the way that a master sommelier would analyse
a mouthful of Château Lafite. Though to extend the analogy, most
of us couldn't bring ourselves to spit it out when we were finished.
No, we would swallow it and hold our glasses out for more, because
we knew that more would inevitably be coming.

Probably, we had become addicted to the moral victories, and we
would have great difficulty in adjusting to life without them, if that
day ever came.

So we had savoured that 2-2 draw with Belgium downstairs in the
International Bar, our base camp close to the offices of *Hot Press* for

whom I did most of my work at the time, because it had featured an ingredient none of us had ever encountered before.

It wasn't just the fact that Ireland equalised twice, away from home, against a team which had reached the semi-final of the last World Cup — we had always had the fighting spirit — it was the fact that the second equaliser had come so late in the game: generally, we didn't 'do' late equalisers. Late equalisers were done to us.

And it had come from a penalty, which was quite extraordinary, really, after all that we had been through. And the penalty had been a gift presented to us by the Belgian keeper, Jean-Marie Pfaff, who had made a lunatic charge which upended Frank Stapleton in a position in which he had seemed most unlikely to score.

All of these things, coming together, had left us high on the improbability of it all.

It was on that night, that I first heard the line that Jack Charlton must be one of Napoleon's 'lucky generals'. It would later become such a common line that it would even filter through to the panellists on *Questions and Answers*, the line that the quality which Napoleon most desired in his generals was that they be lucky. But I had first heard it said by Bill Graham, my old *Hot Press* colleague and mentor — Bill was also U2's mentor, in fact, he was everyone's mentor, if they had any sense — in the International Bar on the night that Jean-Marie Pfaff crazily gave us the penalty which was scored with thoroughbred conviction by Liam Brady.

There was a distinct sense of novelty about this … this 'luck' thing … and we didn't quite know how to deal with it. But we were back on familiar ground anyway by the time the Group was being wound up with Bulgaria playing Scotland at home. A win for Scotland would get us to Germany 88 — but it seemed certain that whatever luck we had had, there wouldn't be enough of it to see us through.

We would watch the formalities of the match in Sofia anyway, because someone had to. And we probably had nothing better to do than sit up at the counter of the International on a very grey afternoon in November, supping pints and watching football and waiting for something good to happen.

By 'we', here, I don't mean the Irish nation as a whole and certainly not the Olé Olé nation or the corporate nation or the *Q&A* nation, just a few loyalists such as myself and my friends Arthur Mathews, who would later co-write *Father Ted* and *I, Keano*, and the controversial rock journalist George Byrne. And Con Houlihan was down in Bambrick's of Portobello. He has written of this grey day, bringing us the lovely image of the owner's dog snoozing in front of the fire.

There was no-one banging a bodhrán, dressed as a leprechaun. Big Jack himself had gone fishing. In the International, we had to ask for the telly to be turned on, and it was just a telly, not a big screen. There was nothing big about this. There was considerably more interest in the recent demise of Eamonn Andrews than in the inevitable demise of the Republic's latest effort — our most celebrated broadcaster would only die once: the Republic would die many times.

After a while we weren't really watching it, we were just 'keeping a watching brief', as they say. Bulgaria had an awe-inspiring record at home in Sofia, an achievement which was embellished by legends of referees loudly consorting in their hotel rooms with state-sponsored Bulgarian prostitutes, but somehow none the less impressive for all that. As for Scotland, we knew that they were capable of anything. They could beat Brazil and then they could lose to Liechtenstein, for no reason except that they were Scotland. In them, too, there is a deep restlessness of the soul.

But by the looks of it, they clearly weren't going to be doing anything perverse in Sofia, on this day.

Then something good happened. Colette Rooney came in from *Hot Press*, just up the road, to ask me if I could go to London the following day to interview Robbie Robertson. Of course I could. The former mainman with The Band had just released a solo album, which contained at least two wonderful tracks, 'Somewhere Down The Crazy River', and 'Fallen Angel', which could stand alongside his classic cuts such as 'The Weight', and 'The Shape I'm In', and 'The Night They Drove Old Dixie Down'. I revere The Band above all others, and to meet Robbie Robertson himself would be a signal honour.

And then Scotland scored.

It is not true to say that everyone in Ireland remembers where they were when Gary Mackay of Hearts, winning his first cap, scored that goal for Scotland with four minutes to go. Because like I said, the only people actually involved at this end were a few lost souls scattered around the country and Bambrick's dog.

What they also forget, is the agony that was yet to come. Brutalised by the abuse inflicted on us over the years, despite George Hamilton's now-frenzied commentary, we were loath to even celebrate that goal until we saw with our own eyes that they were kicking off again at the centre circle.

So many times, it seemed, we had seen good goals for the Republic disallowed, we had lost hope that there was even the most rudimentary form of justice at work in this football world. Joy had turned to disappointment so many times, we didn't bother with the joy any more.

For years we couldn't properly celebrate a goal until we had something akin to forensic proof that the referee had allowed it, that all the paperwork had been done and everyone had signed off on it.

We had instant recall of some of the bleaker legends of Irish football, such as the times Frank Stapleton had vital goals disallowed against Belgium in Brussels and against France in Paris for no reason, or at least none that was vaguely plausible. Had there even been an Irish goal disallowed for no reason on this very ground in Sofia, a long time ago?

So even though this Scotland goal was being allowed to stand, it seemed inconceivable to us that another four minutes of normal time and God knows how long of injury time could go by without it all being taken away from us, in some uniquely twisted manner.

This is what Ireland had done to us.

This is the way we were, near the end of the 1980s. Not just the football, but all the other bullshit, the wrecked economy, the divorce referendum and the abortion referendum, the North, everything that was done under the colours of green, white and gold, had eventually worn us down to this level. We were sick men. Anyone who made it out of here had made it despite all the bullshit, driven by a desperate desire to be free of the bullshit.

It became strangely forgotten during the era of the Tiger, but as I recall, one of the more influential events of the late 1980s was the publication of a book by Professor Joe Lee, *Ireland 1912–1985: Politics and Society.*

Again, because we got locked into that bullshit narrative of success breeding success, we overlooked the fact that failure was also a powerful motivator, and that we had it in spades.

This book, which was a surprise best-seller, was essentially a long and detailed history of failure in Ireland since the foundation of the State. The author was then Professor of Modern History at UCC, a man who could increasingly be heard on RTÉ radio explaining how everything in Ireland was broken.

Clearly he was a man who loved his country, and who was scrupulously, even obsessively fair, about what had been done right, and what had been done wrong. He gave respect where it was due. You would feel at times that he almost gave too much respect, even where it wasn't due. But if anything, his well-known even-handedness made his book even more important and powerful and depressing — this guy wasn't saying this stuff for effect, he was saying it because it was true, and he could prove it.

Little wonder that so many of us bought his book, but so few of us had the heart to read it.

But we would hear those who had been able to read it all the way through speaking in solemn tones about the sadness of it all. About Ireland, and how we had done so many things so badly compared with similar countries, who had somehow worked out how to govern themselves in a vaguely intelligent and responsible fashion.

All who heard this drank deep and were silent.

That big book felt like an epitaph for the whole doomed project that was the Republic of Ireland, one that was superbly and lovingly crafted in itself, but an epitaph all the same, for something dead and gone. Lee stopped short of saying that we should just hand the country back to whoever we got it from and say sorry about all that. But to many, that was the only reasonable conclusion to be drawn.

So that's roughly where we were, near the end of the 1980s in Ireland, without even venturing towards the badlands of inter-national football and the men who had been forging our destinies in that regard. Throw in the FAI, described by writer Michael Nugent as 'a perpetually exploding clown's car', and various Bulgarian hookers and so forth, and you get a sense of what we were up against here.

Which is how, in the International Bar on 11 November 1987, even though this extraordinary thing had happened, with Scotland scoring so late in the game, we were convinced that it could only be the precursor to some grotesque denouement. We were already steeling ourselves for it, as the Bulgarians were now playing with a wild urgency, the blackguards, startled out of their cynical torpor by the unthinkable event which had just befallen them.

Sportingly, if insanely, a Scot had rushed to retrieve the ball from the net after the goal, a goal that wouldn't have happened if the ref had stopped play for a bad Bulgarian foul in the build-up.

Their captain, Nasko Sirakov, sent a shot from the edge of the area which seemed certain to squeeze inside the far post, but which somehow went wide. The equaliser was coming. We knew it was coming. We cursed this savage new twist, this cruel raising of our hopes.

Then Arthur Mathews came up with a formula, which seemed to make it bearable. 'There's about three minutes to go, including injury time,' he said. 'That's about as long as "Teenage Kicks" by The Undertones.' Which wasn't long at all really, since he put it like that. And so myself, George and Arthur, in the privacy of our own tormented heads, 'played' that record by the Undertones, that three minutes of pop perfection which itself had been forged against a backdrop of pain and terror.

————

When it was over, the RTÉ studio had become a place of madness.

John Giles was there, Maurice Setters and Mick McCarthy.

Jack couldn't be found.

Gone fishing.

He couldn't be phoned, faxed or texted, and even when these technologies became more common, Jack was not the sort of guy to be checking his messages when he had gone fishing. Avoiding any flak that might have come his way when we didn't qualify, he was now missing his moment of triumph, yet acquiring just a little more mystique in the process. What other manager in world football would be incommunicado on such a day?

Arthur and George and I went downstairs to our usual spot in the International, where the real drinking could commence. Already I could tell that I would be severely hung over for Robbie Robertson, but then he is a great artist and a great humanitarian, who would be no stranger to men in that condition.

I did not care.

We were still there at closing time at 11 o'clock on the 11th of November.

It was the eleventh hour of the eleventh day of the eleventh month.

Chapter 2 ~

THE PHONE IN THE HALL

Bob Geldof was my landlord at the time. That would be Bob Senior, father of famous Bob, who owned a large Edwardian house on Crosthwaite Park in Dun Laoghaire divided into flats. Liam Mackey, my friend from *Hot Press*, lived in the basement flat and when he moved upstairs to a slightly larger premises, I moved in to the basement along with Jane — our baby Roseanne would soon be born.

He was a lovely man, old Geldof, still kicking around the world in a camper van which young Bob had bought for him. We were paying him more than we'd been paying for the olde worlde flat in Leinster Road in Rathmines where we had been living, but Dun Laoghaire had distinct advantages such as the nearby DART, which, it was increasingly felt, might not be such a bad idea after all. And there was Dun Laoghaire itself, where we now had characters such as Barry Devlin, formerly of Horslips, in the neighbourhood, as well as Sonny Condell, who played at the first rock gig I ever attended, wearing the first pair of leather trousers I had ever seen, in the Dean Crowe Hall in Athlone. He'd been supporting Peggy's Leg. In Rathmines, we had had Father Michael Cleary living across the road.

I was now working for a national newspaper — soon I would be working for two national newspapers and a national magazine. Yet it seemed quite normal to be renting not just the flat, but the television in the flat.

'Confidence', in Ireland at that time, was such a fragile thing.

Eoghan Corry, then Features Editor of the *Irish Press*, had asked me to write a TV column for the paper, making use of the rented TV (I think I bought the pen and paper outright). I would soon start contributing to the *Sunday Independent* and there was still *Hot Press* — in fact, I had interviewed Jack for that paper, early in the campaign for Euro 88.

I had been writing a sports column called 'Foul Play' in which we were placing football in a rock 'n' roll context long before Nick Hornby and *Fever Pitch*. So an interview with Jack or with any football man would be a normal procedure, if indeed the word 'normal' could ever be used in relation to a *Hot Press* interview — for example, we used to actually print most of things that people said, rather than observing the ancient journalistic conventions of tidying up the bad language and the digressions and the loose talk in general. We did not feel that the people needed to be protected from such things.

The interview was done in the lounge of an airport hotel, with physio and batman Mick Byrne scurrying around organising room-keys and generally coming across like the PA to a busy executive. Indeed Jack laughed about the male-ness of the world in which he moved, expressing disappointment that I wasn't a woman — Colette from *Hot Press* had organised the interview and he had been expecting her.

He seemed younger that day than we generally remember him. When he became a sort of Father of the Nation a few years later, he assumed an aura of seniority which obscured the fact that when he took the Ireland job in 1986, he was just 50.

For the first time, I noted that he kept getting names wrong: names of players, names of countries; he referred to Bulgaria as Romania and instinctively I was about to correct him, but stopped myself. If he didn't know the difference by now, it didn't matter. And while he was being factually inaccurate, he was not too far from the truth — for what difference was there really between Bulgaria and

Romania? As Con Houlihan put it, these guys from behind the Iron Curtain who would come over to play football, were ultimately doing it for 'the bit of freedom and some decent food'.

In fact, I don't know what Colette had said to him, but Jack was ready to talk about environmental issues, too, which I felt at the time was surprisingly generous to a magazine that he'd probably never heard of, and about which Mick Byrne, with his local knowledge, might have had some legitimate concerns.

He spoke with passion about various fish-kills which were happening at that time. Fish-kills were big in Ireland in the 1980s, most of them caused by farmers releasing vast quantities of slurry into rivers and lakes which were once pristine fishing grounds but which were now destroyed. He argued that farmers found guilty of such hooliganism should have the land taken away from them.

Naturally, I would write up this interview in longhand, on sheets of foolscap. Because we wrote such long interviews at *Hot Press* and because most of us were little more than children, our typing skills hadn't developed to a stage where we could rattle off 3,000 words to deadline. In fact, the practice of writing in longhand would remain with me for many years, almost until the turn of the century, even when I had learned to type properly — I had become so used to thinking in longhand, I felt that a piece always read a bit better if I wrote it up first and then typed it.

To recall the methods we used at the time at what we assumed to be the cutting edge of the media, is to realise that despite our modern notions about getting football managers from England and the like, we were still not far removed from medieval ways.

When I first started writing for the *Irish Press* and then the *Sunday Independent*, where typed copy was a minimum requirement, Jane would do the typing for me and I would carry the precious sheets down to the DART. I would read through them on the train, crossing things out and adding things in with a biro. I would hand this attractive offering to Anne Harris in the *Indo*, or to Eoghan Corry at the *Press*.

I didn't say 'in' the *Press*, because I would always meet Eoghan, who was one of the gentlemen of the game, in Mulligan's of Poolbeg Street. I would have a pint of Fürstenberg and he might have a pint of Guinness, and he would read my article there in the pub and hopefully at some point he would start laughing or otherwise indicate his approval. Then Eoghan would take my copy up to the office and he would be gone for a while, editing his features. But soon he would return and we would have a few more pints of Fürstenberg and maybe a few more pints of Guinness and a few more laughs.

It seems now that the newspaper business in Ireland was run amid a veritable Niagara of alcohol. An angry reader once wrote to Eoghan complaining about something in the *Irish Press* which had annoyed him, giving an address which indicated that he was an inmate of a mental institution. In fact he stated in his letter, 'As you can see from my address, I am mentally disturbed'.

Eoghan wrote back to him, under the *Irish Press* letterhead, with the opening line: 'As you can see from our address, we, too, are mentally disturbed.'

And yet, fantastically, it seemed to work. Two newspapers a day and a third on Sunday somehow emerged from Burgh Quay, along with a lot of interesting people of the kind that you don't find any more in 'the media', in these good-living times. To quote Houlihan again, the modern newspaper office has all the atmosphere of a suburban pharmacy.

Not only were they interesting, as I look back on it, but I marvel at the general levels of kindness and understanding which these highly experienced professionals displayed towards the likes of me, arriving into their world without their ancient skills such as short-hand, and without much intention of learning it either.

And we didn't have a phone in the flat. The phone was in the hall, one of the old black pay-phones, with Button A and Button B on it. Jane and I and Roseanne were at the back and the hall was round the front, so you would hear it ringing in the distance and if no-one had answered it after three or four rings, this would mean that Liam wasn't in, and if it kept ringing, it meant that other tenants such as Pat McManus, the lead guitarist with the heavy metal band Mama's Boys, weren't in either. At which point you would run like hell to answer it, out the back and round the front.

Astonishing though it now seems, while journalists at the time were inclined to chide Jack for his supposed lack of tactical sophistication, we didn't regard it as abnormal to be living in flats with no phones.

Perhaps the defining narrative of the phone-in-the-hall era concerns an interview with Keith Richards which was due to be conducted by Liam Fay of *Hot Press*, over the phone, with Liam at his flat in Rathmines and Keith at his home in the Caribbean.

Except Keith's people obviously wouldn't be giving the private Caribbean phone number of a member of the Rolling Stones to some Paddy rock journalist. So it was arranged that Keith would be given Liam Fay's number, which he would call at 7.30 in the evening.

But Liam didn't have a phone in the flat.

The phone was in the hall.

So it was, that one evening at around 7 o'clock in a large old house in Rathmines, Liam Fay knocked on the door of every tenant in the building and asked them if they could do him a favour and avoid using the phone at around 7.30, because he was expecting a call from Keith Richards in the Caribbean.

———

So in my mid-twenties, while I seemed to have something resembling a career, even a life, it would not have crossed my mind that this might be the time to do something mad like get a mortgage and live in an actual house of our own. We had a powerful stereo and a fine record collection and some very good books and we could always do the Lotto, which had just started. So we didn't feel the need to be borrowing, say, 50 grand, to get on the 'property ladder'.

Most of us who came of age during the 1980s were similarly indifferent to the long term, just happy enough to get through the week with the rent paid. And most of the people I knew just drank too much to be annoying themselves with property ladders and the like. We were already angry enough, about things like divorce and contraception and abortion, not because we cared much for these things in themselves, but because they were the issues in the moral civil war being fought in Ireland, which Jack may not have noticed in his zeal to show us how to win football matches, but which was still festering.

Not that it's necessarily a bad thing, to be angry, if you're working in journalism. It was probably what brought many of us into it in the first place, this idea that there was an old Ireland to be defeated, as quickly and as completely as we could manage it, to break through the delusions which had sustained that old Ireland, the lies which were just too big, even for Paddy.

When people enter 'the media' now, they have all sorts of fine ambitions to review restaurants for the *Irish Times*, or to write a wine column for the *Sunday Business Post*, or to present the weather on TV3. For us, presenting the weather was an impossible dream — at least until Ireland was free. Living in Dun Laoghaire, for example, it would occur to me, as I watched the boat leaving for Holyhead every day, that roughly ten of the passengers on board must be women heading off to get an abortion. Given that 3,000 women at the very least were doing this each year, and that, pre-Ryanair, most of them would get the boat, you just did the math.

But there was no abortion in Ireland, so that was all right. We were not like the others, who permitted the slaughter of the innocents.

Though of course we were like the others, we just pretended that we weren't, out-sourcing our abortions for decades, the way we had out-sourced anything else we couldn't handle, to England.

It was these fantastic feats of self-deception that were being challenged at the time. It was nominally about these great moral issues, but it was ultimately about Paddy trying to blast through some of the bullshit, the terrible, terrible bullshit in which he had been standing up to his neck for generations.

So while the 1980s were a hateful time in many ways, they may eventually be viewed in a kinder light, as bullshit's last stand.

A certain kind of bullshit, at least.

Ultimately, we would still have ample quantities of it knocking around, and varieties yet to be discovered. It is a national addiction, which can manifest itself in many ways. And of course it is not un-related to our primary addiction, the same then, as it is now, and which unites so many of us in alcoholic fellowship, wandering unsteadily to the beat of the same drum.

So when a load of cant by Bishop Brendan Comiskey appeared in a Church publication, accusing me of blasphemy in relation to something I had written in the *Irish Press*, it merely confirmed to me that people like him were the enemy and that they must be done down.

We had just about reached the stage when a 'blasphemer' wouldn't lose his job and have to leave the country after being set upon by a bishop, and soon Bishop Eamon Casey would be doing his own bit to advance the liberal agenda. But I still could have done without Comiskey's ambush over one line that I hadn't even intended to be blasphemous — and anyway, it wasn't much of a line, something about Madonna the singer possibly having a child, who will hopefully give her less trouble than the original Madonna had with her child.

I would condemn myself for heavy-handedness and for the all-round lameness of that effort and I ask God's forgiveness for that. Nuala O'Faolain defended me in the *Irish Times*, mercifully declaring that she wouldn't mention the offending line because it was so innocuous, sparing both the zealots and myself a lot of grief.

It took me a long time to realise that Comiskey and I may have had our differences over some minor matters of theology, but that in relation to the one true faith — the beer — we were more or less *ad idem*. Comiskey was eventually treated for alcoholism, though at the time, when there was not even a mild suspicion about his weakness for the jar, he would have been regarded as one of the more able administrators in Ireland, with newspaper profiles suggesting that if he hadn't gone for the priesthood, he would have undoubtedly become one of our more progressive business leaders.

———

Our best and best-loved footballer, Paul McGrath, would also eventually be treated for alcoholism, though at the time, we were only worried about his knees. It would become a national euphemism, Paul McGrath's knees, somewhat complicated by the fact that he really had a problem with his knees, but that problem tended to be aggravated by his drinking. In fact, Paul was drinking steadily — and so was I — on the night we agreed that I would write his biography.

Alcoholism, they say, is a 'progressive' disease. Along the way there are mysterious lines that you cross without knowing it, which only start to become clear to you when it is all over — if it is all over. If you could measure it on a scale of one to ten, on the night that I agreed to write Paul McGrath's biography, in the run-up to Euro 88, I was probably at about six. By the end of the Charlton era, I would be up there at about eight-and-a-half, pushing nine, and in truth, I probably never went beyond that — you don't need to, really.

Where was Big Paul at? Only he knows, and maybe he still can't quite work it out.

But it was quite a night, all the same.

The Boys In Green, as they were now increasingly known, were down in Windmill Lane Studios recording the track 'The Boys In Green', which would be their anthem for Germany, and which was written by a gentleman of the press, the late Mick Carwood.

We are the Boys in Green
The best you've ever seen
We've just made history-ee
We're off to German-ee
We've had to wait till now
Big Jack has shown us how
You'll wonder where we've been
When you see the Boys in Green

And you'll say Ireland, Ireland, show them what we've got
Ireland, Ireland we can beat this lot
Ireland, Ireland we can celebrate
Ireland, Ireland in Euro 88

———

We should pause here and try to imagine an English football journalist contributing to the England cause in this fashion, and try though we might, we just can't see it.

His song was produced on that Sunday afternoon in Windmill Lane by Paul Brady and featured many of the Boys themselves, who sang heartily all the way through, observed by other gentlemen of the press including myself, Mr George Byrne and Mr Eamon Carr.

I recall talking at length to Chris Hughton, about how he, a black man, had always regarded himself as Irish. He seemed patently sincere and he had nothing to prove in that regard anyway, since he had been a black man playing for Ireland back in the days when we only had about five black men in the entire country — and by 1988 that number hadn't increased to any noticeable extent.

Indeed George Byrne happened to be on a trip to Detroit around that time, with friends, and the taxi-driver, learning they were from Ireland, asked them how many of 'the brothers' were in Ireland. And they started going through them … 'there's Paul McGrath … and Philo, of course, but he's dead now … and Kevin Sharkey … and Dave Murphy … and … and that guy who plays the guitar outside Bewleys …'

The taxi-driver interjected. 'That many, huh?'

But one of them was Paul McGrath, after all, who contained multitudes.

When the recording party repaired to the Dockers pub next door to Windmill, Eamon Carr and George Byrne and I found ourselves in the corner of the lounge, drinking with Paul and his companion, John Anderson, of Newcastle Utd and Ireland. It was Eamon that Paul really wanted to talk to, Eamon being a *bona fide* Irish rock legend from his time with Horslips. I myself probably would not have been sitting there if it wasn't for the same Horslips and the life-changing effect that they had had on me and on a fair few others like me in 'rural Ireland', lonely boys, out on the weekend.

We lived only for their all-too-infrequent visits. They were magical, extraordinary, these five men, who were able to demonstrate that you could be playing the dancehalls like a thousand other Irish bands and yet somehow not be bad.

That you could write your own songs, and they would not be bad.

That you could put on a show and it would not be bad, but would have wondrous things like a proper PA system and a mixing desk and actual roadies darting around the stage, plugging in guitars which, when played, would not be bad.

Eamon was one of my heroes, too.

And as the talk inevitably turned to Ireland and the state that she was in, Paul was getting stuck in to his own upbringing, how Ireland had treated him, and soon there was a fine and righteous anger around that table.

I had only encountered Paul once before that, when I had been coming out of the International Bar and had almost run into him and a woman with whom he seemed to be arguing. You'd never hear him giving interviews.

So this was the first time I realised what an articulate fellow he was, how well he seemed to understand the things that he had seen. And as the pint pots stacked up in the Dockers, he said that he wanted to put all this stuff in a book, all this shocking stuff.

Thus, for a couple of hours one night long ago in the Dockers pub, I became Paul McGrath's official biographer.

He meant it, and I meant it.

We meant it with all our hearts.

Our agreement was witnessed by a distinguished if controversial rock journalist and a genuine Irish rock legend, so it was sound.

On the way out the door, in a state of high excitement, Paul gave me his telephone number in Manchester, written on a scrap of paper.

I said I would make that call.

Of course I would make that call.

I never made that call. For days, for weeks afterwards, I would look at that number and know deep down that I could not make that call. Because even when we are starting to get lost in the fog of alcohol, there is some voice that calls us back.

At some level that I didn't really comprehend at the time, I still knew that when a man is out drinking and he starts making elaborate plans, and he makes a certain commitment, he doesn't necessarily mean it. Even if he says on the night: 'I mean it'. Especially if he says on the night: 'I mean it'.

And that voice which called me back was a good voice, a protective voice. Because of course the book that Paul and I would have produced at the time, given our mutual state of awareness about the way we were, would have been a tad, shall we say, incomplete.

The autobiography he would eventually produce with Vincent Hogan would become one of the most successful Irish sports books of all time. It would tell the story of a man who was coming to accept his powerlessness over alcohol. But that would be nearly twenty years later, when Paul was ready for it. In the run-up to Euro 88, he wasn't ready for it. And I wasn't ready for it.

Which was not something I knew for sure at the time, just an intuition that stopped me making that call.

I'm sure that Paul understood, in fact I know that he did, because I would go on to interview him for *Hot Press* at the zenith of the Charlton years.

It was still a rare thing for him to be interviewed, but he seemed to be in a good place that day in Bloom's Hotel. He revealed that Jack used to call him 'John', perhaps confusing him with John McGrath, who was the Southampton centre-half when Jack was a player. He joked about his knees. Indeed …

He never mentioned that ghost biography, and neither did I. Since he had agreed to do the interview it seemed self-evident that he had lost no sleep over it.

But I wonder, I wonder … if we'd had mobile phones back in 1988, or even a land-line in the flat, I wonder if I'd have made that call. And to what madness it might have led us.

There is something to be said after all, for the phone in the hall.

Chapter 3

THE RE-UNIFICATION OF IRELAND

They kept calling him a gruff Yorkshireman, but Jack Charlton wasn't from Yorkshire at all, but from Northumberland. Famously, along with Jack and his brother Bobby, the north-east mining town of Ashington had produced the Milburns, an illustrious football family related to the Charltons, and which included the celebrated Newcastle Utd centre-forward Jackie Milburn, 'Wor Jackie'.

The Charltons were much closer to that Geordie tradition than to the gruff Yorkshire mould into which Jack had been placed by so many of his new admirers.

It may be just that irresistible urge to embrace the cliché, but in Ireland, we think we're better than that.

Not that Jack himself would give a monkey's, but we pride ourselves on knowing more about England than England knows about us. Thus if, say, Roy Keane were to be routinely described in the British media as a Kerryman, we would shake our heads sadly at this new nadir in tabloid vulgarity. Because we would know that these are not minor matters; that for a very long time, we have been obsessed with these questions of who we are and what we are and where we're coming from.

The first thing that Paddy says to Paddy when they meet on foreign soil, is 'what part are you from?' We have a deep understanding of these matters of identity as they relate to ourselves, but beyond that, apparently we lose interest.

Our self-absorption is that of a teenager, as is natural for the citizens of a young country. And our self-esteem has never been the best. In fact, as I learned more about the nature of addiction, I came across a definition which has a haunting resonance for anyone with a drop of Irish blood in them — big ego, low self-esteem is the classic combination, the essential duality in the psyche of the alcoholic.

Big ego … low self-esteem. Ah, yes, that would ring a few bells, for Paddy.

So right from the start, our love for Paul McGrath was no doubt partly rooted in this profound intuition, this sixth sense that he had the 'weakness' which so many of us have. And that withal, he was magnificent.

And then it got a bit tricky, because even though the true story of Paul McGrath had not yet been told, we probably knew enough at that stage to realise that he was magnificent *despite* his Irishness, and all that had happened to him on this side of the Irish Sea. Deep down, we were guilty that we could do so little for such a vulnerable kid, that England at least could provide him with a stage on which he could display his great gifts.

Though lest we forget, if Ireland had abused him, England in turn had abused Ireland. Always, there was the get-out clause.

We had had this uniquely twisted relationship with Johnny England for a very long time, until the wonders of the Charlton years forced us to move away somewhat from the comforting simplicities of old and to realise that maybe, just maybe, we could handle the truth. Which, as was suggested by another Irishman who did rather well for himself in England, is 'rarely pure and never simple'.

We were in Germany now, with England beaten at their own game.

But how could we have done it without them? This defining moment in our island story had been granted to us, not by our Gaelic football and the amateur ethos of which we are so proud. Not by our hurling, which is 'the fastest team sport in the world', and not by our handball, or anything else that might be played in the environs of Croke Park. It was all down to association football, the game of the conqueror and the coloniser; and the man in charge, trying to correct some of our ancient inadequacies, was a 'gruff Yorkshireman'.

Likewise, it was a bookie from Belfast, Barney Eastwood, who steered Barry McGuigan to the world title in boxing, again not one of our Gaelic games, but which kept us going anyway during McGuigan's glorious run.

In fact, Euro 88 came just a year after the astounding achievements of Stephen Roche, who came apparently out of nowhere (Dundrum actually) to win the Tour de France, the Giro d'Italia and the World road race Championship, all in 1987.

Again, his efforts had owed virtually nothing to the traditions of the Gael, apart from the tradition of getting the hell out of here if you're any good.

I had heard of Sean Kelly, because of a highly-regarded book about him by the sports writer David Walsh, but Roche meant nothing to me when, as *Hot Press* roving ambassador to the world of sport, I arrived to interview him very early one morning, placing my absurdly large cassette recorder on the table in front of him, while he breakfasted in a hotel in the borough of Dun Laoghaire, shortly before he and the rest of his fellow cyclists started the journey to Cork.

In fact, the extent of my knowledge can be gauged by my incredulity at his proposed schedule, this idea which he had casually voiced, whereby they would cycle *all the way* from Dublin to Cork.

'You mean ... you'll actually cycle ... all the way?'

'Well, if the wind is against us, we might drive to Portlaoise and just take it from there', he said.

Good luck with that, I thought.

'By the way, could you not have brought a bigger tape-recorder?' he quipped, with that understated wit which would become so familiar to us all a year later.

For now, it was all just a bit baffling, especially at such an early hour.

And anyway it was only cycling, about which I was no more ignorant than any other Irish person, little knowing that soon we would be speaking sagely about the *peloton* and the *echelon* and forming considered opinions about the abilities of various *domestiques*. But I remember being impressed, as the photographer took the pictures, at the way Roche insisted on getting all his sponsorship logos together before the snapper did his thing. Yes, the interview might have been a waste of time, but the picture would make it vaguely worth his while.

You could tell he'd been abroad, to be so attuned to the commercial realities of modern sport. That he had left Paddy behind on the Sally Gap in this regard. The Boys In Green, in these early days, would be drinking all night with journalists, expecting nothing in return expect perhaps the vague prospect that one of them might write his autobiography, or spending the afternoon singing in Windmill Lane for no great reward except perhaps its knock-on benefit for squad morale. The players singing 'The Boys In Green' on the *Late Late Show*, for all the world like a bunch of well-meaning lads from the pub down the road who had got this thing together to pay for an operation for a sick child is one of the more poignant images of that time — but a step up from the night when Gay Byrne announced, 'I have just been handed a piece of paper here which says that Jack Charlton has been appointed manager of Ireland — whatever that means'.

Roche, his jersey plastered with the logos which he insisted be in place before any pictures would be taken, had left us all behind. And we revered him for it, gathering in multitudes in the centre of

Dublin to welcome him home from the Tour de France, where he had stood on the podium on the Champs Élysées with the paws of our Taoiseach all over him, claiming credit where none was due.

Again, Roche had performed his miracles despite being Irish, where his sport had had a storied past but no future at the time he emerged from the suburb of Dundrum, radiating class. It was the French on that occasion who supplied the training and the stage and whatever else you needed to get yourself up the Alpe d'Huez and into the yellow jersey.

But usually it was Johnny England who made our sporting wishes come true. Whether we liked it or not, the English first division had for decades been regarded as the natural destination of the most talented Irish ball-players. And support for English football ran deep in the cities of Dublin and Cork and the garrison towns too, and beyond — I grew up in the garrison town of Athlone in the 1970s, when almost everyone in my school had a natural affinity with Leeds or Liverpool or Man Utd.

But the country lads weren't exactly immune to the attractions of association football either. What Jack did, with the results he achieved, was the popularisation of football in Ireland, beyond this hard core of aficionados which had always existed. And in so doing, with the primitive style which he favoured, he alienated the football men, the people who had always loved the game and kept it going.

Jack certainly didn't bring football to a new level in Ireland, at least not in a good way, but he brought the popularity of football to a level whereby Gaelic matches were cancelled because they clashed with World Cup matches and English football, as represented by the Premier League, has arguably become our *de facto* national sport.

You could suggest that the GAA has obvious merits as a 'community' organisation, but equally, on the sporting side, it actually demands a lot less of its followers than the English game. A Kerryman would get away with not making a trip to Dublin until the

All-Ireland final, an extraordinarily light load to bear, when you consider that the same Kerryman, if he supports Liverpool, would be giving his full attention to at least two games a week from the month of August through to the following May. And then there are the Leinster hurling finals with Croke Park only one-quarter full, because Kilkenny fans don't suppose their team will be needing them yet.

Certainly the GAA provides a few big days out, generally in fine weather, but 'the ban' on its members from playing foreign games, a ban that was only lifted in 1971, showed that sport in itself was not necessarily the GAA's main priority, that it was also a political and cultural movement which defined the nation in a narrow and dis-criminatory fashion, which was perversely against the national interest. The GAA concocted a kind of sporting version of the Iron Curtain, behind which the purity of the Gaelic project could be maintained without interference from the more decadent culture on the other side. And it banished all dissidents.

It was indeed one of Bill Graham's more inspired moments when, in another context, he described the old Soviet Union as being 'like an entire continent run by the GAA'. He was right at the time, but if Bill had lived to see the new Croke Park, with 'soccer' matches being played in it, he would doubtless have reviewed his position. He would have acknowledged that like the Soviet Union, eventually the GAA had its *glasnost* and *perestroika*. And unlike the GAA, the Soviet Union could only manage it with a President who was blind drunk most of the time.

And there was always the amateur ethos, a positive off-shoot of this generally twisted old attitude. It can be regarded as Paddy's special contribution to sport in a world mad for money. Paddy can be in Sydney or Chicago looking at the All-Ireland final in which none of the stars are being paid a weekly wage, and he can be thinking: we are indeed a great sporting nation. That's the 'big ego' bit there. But there is also a little voice which nags at him, a voice reminding him that this is, after all, an exclusively Irish affair, and that if these guys are as great as they're cracked up to be, they'd surely be across in England playing the old garrison game, making millions.

That's the 'low self-esteem' bit.

Like, we may be a great sporting nation, blah blah, but are we actually any good? And if we are, how can we tell if we never compete with people from other countries?

Gaelic games were at once a comfort blanket and a source of insecurity at the time of Euro 88. They allowed Paddy to demonstrate many of the things that he did very well. But was sport one of these things? There had been a few iconic individuals — Christy O'Connor the golfer; Ronnie Delany the runner; a few rugby players who may have been nominally Irish but who in truth belonged to an upper-middle-class élite which was beyond nationality; there were a number of phenomenal horses and jockeys and trainer Vincent O'Brien; Eddie Macken the show-jumper; Barry McGuigan and the boxers who always did their stuff at the Olympics; Sean Kelly and Stephen Roche …

There was strength and depth, in Paddy's sporting contribution, but alas, the one that really counted was the one that had always eluded us.

Association Football, the garrison game, is the one that counts. The rest is not exactly bullshit, but football is the one which gives everyone a chance, simply because it is played everywhere and it doesn't require a set of golf clubs or a place at a fee-paying school, or a horse. And it certainly doesn't require you to be from the 32 counties of Ireland, to know what's going on.

Jack Charlton would become quite fond of the big days out at Croke Park, though, as a typical 'gruff Yorkshireman', he would bravely express reservations about any sport which is played in just one country in the entire world. He would also marvel at what he perceived to be the lowly status of football in Ireland, by comparison with these so-called national sports of Gaelic football and hurling and greyhound racing.

But here he revealed that perhaps he didn't know us that well after all.

Which is reasonable enough, since we don't know ourselves that well either. He didn't seem to fully understand, as he sat on a fine day in Croke Park with the stadium full, enjoying the spectacle along with the great and the good and maybe even the followers of Kerry or Kilkenny who could now actually be arsed to come to Dublin in person, that it's not like this all the time. That the Irish were probably as good at football as they were at any other sport. Perhaps better, when you reflect on the numbers of high-class individuals who had gone to England and had successful careers.

There was a man called Peter Molloy who owned a pub in Athlone when I was growing up, who had played for Aston Villa in the 1950s. He was part of a steady exodus of 'good professionals'. And then there were players of the very highest order, such as John Giles, Jackie Carey, Liam Whelan, Tony Dunne, Paul McGrath, Ronnie Whelan, Brady and O'Leary and Stapleton. There were just never enough of them out there at the same time. And even if there had been, their best efforts would no doubt have been thwarted by the machinations of the FAI, the dysfunctional sporting body that other dysfunctional sporting bodies call 'the galácticos'.

So Paddy was perhaps bringing a tad more of his native genius to this than Jack seemed to realise. And now it turned out that there was more of it out there than either of them had realised. Not that Jack ultimately gave a damn where the players were coming from as long as they did what they were told.

But for us, the 'great-grandmother' rule was about a lot more than fleshing out the squad with useful players. It was a thing of extraordinary psychic and cultural and historical significance. It had

been born out of guilt and shame, this provision in the Irish constitution whereby the children of emigrants could become Irish
citizens. It seemed to be saying to the 'diaspora' that we could do
nothing for them except wave goodbye as they left the country, but
if their children were mad enough to want to come back here, we
wouldn't keep them out. In fact, our citizenship laws back in the
1950s were partly influenced by the number of Irish women who
were having illegitimate children in England because they were
afraid to have them in Ireland.

And there was the ever-present hint of bullshit too, because we
knew that the overwhelming majority of those who left Ireland
would never return.

Many of them would get married happily or unhappily in
England, but never unhappily enough, it seemed, to risk the boat
back. Their children would include the likes of Johnny Rotten and
Shane MacGowan and the Gallaghers of Oasis and all four members
of The Smiths, who would enrich the cultural life of England while
still maintaining a sort of Irishness. But on the whole, no good had
come to the mother country from this long-standing arrangement,
apart from the relief of getting rid of a few more unfortunates whom
the Irish economy was unable to support.

And there was always America, which was now taking in the Irish
in numbers which would ensure a full house for Christy Moore
every night of the year, if he so wished.

But the emigration to England was always the most damning and
the most disgraceful, not just because it involved the old enemy
solving our problems, but because it was so near and yet so far. What
kind of a hole were we running here that they would prefer to be
sleeping rough in Camden Town than to be back in the old country
for which they pined at closing time?

And now, through some strange alignment of the planets — or at
least the planet football — after decades of this guilt and shame,

something happened which would be of benefit to all sides. A serious effort was being made to recruit the likes of Townsend and Houghton and Aldridge, McCarthy and Cascarino, ye gods, the sons and grandsons of emigrants, as swiftly and as legally as possible to the Irish football team.

In Ireland we called it payback for emigration, conveniently ignoring the fact that we probably weren't entitled to any payback. And for these players the association with the Republic would be enormously beneficial to their careers.

Football, which has always been more important than most things in life, had worked a sort of national miracle which politics couldn't, which religion most certainly couldn't — a re-unification of Ireland, the best we were ever going to get.

The arrival of the 'English' players gave the diaspora in general a powerful connection to this team of Jack's, not to mention giving Jack a team which could qualify for the tournaments which had previously eluded it. Dermot Bolger witnessed this at Euro 88, in his play *In High Germany*: 'The crowd joined in, every one of them, from Dublin and Cork, from London and Stockholm. And suddenly I knew this was the only country I still owned, those eleven figures in green shirts, that menagerie of accents pleading with God.'

As for Jack's own Englishness, for us it had become either an amusing irony or just another fast one we had pulled on them, taking on the 'gruff Yorkshireman' who had once applied for the England job and not even received the courtesy of a reply.

Again, we told ourselves what we wanted to hear, that this was the sort of Englishman we could take orders from, a rough-hewn individual, a plain fellow whose tastes were not unlike our own, though he was also about as English as you can be, in the sense of having an unambiguous devotion to Queen and country.

Bigger things were happening for us, with a nation re-discovering a part of itself that had been missing, presumed dead. Discovering these weird new phenomena such as luck, and winning, and being part of something that matters.

Chapter 4 ∿

TEN GREAT ENGLAND DEFEATS

Having said all that … having taken from England the great game of football and taken back the sons that she had nurtured for us and beaten her 1-0 in the opening match of the European Championship, a match which England could have won 5-1, or even 7-2, we did not feel any need to be magnanimous in victory.

The film-maker Alan Parker, when he was over in Dublin making *The Commitments* would be deeply disappointed by the wild rejoicing in the saloons of Ireland when anything remotely bad happened to the England football team. Here was the Englishman, Parker, giving opportunities to talented Irish youngsters, making Ireland look and sound better than it actually was, and generally doing us a big favour. And this is how we showed our appreciation. 'But we support you', he would say plaintively.

Indeed, apart from the more obdurate members of the National Front, most England fans would show a benign attitude to the Republic in the big tournaments, even willing them to win, as long as England weren't involved. Which some of us would automatically see as just patronising and just another demonstration of their lack of awareness of the bitter enmity which is supposed to exist between us.

And I do not exclude myself from any of this carry-on. I was able to maintain these apparently contradictory positions, with no feelings of remorse.

At the time I was Anglophile in most things, as were most of the people I knew. We immersed ourselves in English sport and English television and English rock 'n' roll for most of our lives, because we obviously found it better than whatever we were getting at home and yet, how we laughed at Ten Great England Defeats, one of Arthur Mathews' more sublime offerings for *Hot Press*. (Incidentally for the historical record, I should correct the impression that Arthur was a frequent contributor to *Hot Press*. For a long time he was essentially regarded as a lay-out man who just turned out an article from time to time as the mood took him. Here we had one of the best comedy writers in the world, who was only doing it in his spare time — perhaps another sign there of Paddy not pushing himself.)

Christmas would see a new edition of Arthur's 'The Border Fascist', a terrifyingly funny and note-perfect version of a provincial paper, with headlines like 'Belturbet Man Executed in Malaysia', and an ad for hearing aids in Cootehill: 'Are You Fucking Deaf?' And there was the comic strip, 'Charles J. Haughey's Believe It Or Not'.

But the Ten Great England Defeats is what concerns us here. It was the sort of piece that could only have been done by an aficionado, the sort of chap with a suitcase under the bed full of old Drogheda Utd match programmes, someone who knew his football history and who knew England enough to be able to measure out its misery over a period of about 50 years.

There was the catastrophic 1-0 defeat to the United States in the 1950 World Cup ... the 3-2 defeat to Germany in 1970, in the terrible heat of the World Cup quarter-final in Mexico ... the 1-1 draw with Poland at Wembley, which counts as a defeat because it meant England didn't qualify for the 1974 World Cup ... the 2-1 defeat by Argentina in the 1986 World Cup — a scoreline which I heard announced by the captain on a flight from Cork to Dublin, as 'Maradona 2, England 1', to a raucous cheer from all on board. The 1-0 defeat by the Irish in Stuttgart was of course at Number One.

To some extent it is beyond reasoned analysis how those of us who had derived so many of life's pleasures from English sources — Jane McNicholas, the mother of my child, was from England — could be indulging ourselves in this sort of crack. But we will try, anyway, to figure it out.

For once, we can say that this is not a phenomenon that is peculiar to Paddy. Almost all who have had dealings with England seem to take this wild delight in England defeats in any sport. The Australians in particular are able to actually inflict many of these defeats on the cricket pitch, but then it might be argued that Paddy is involved here too, as large numbers of the Aussies can be regarded as Irish in many ways: Paddy-with-the-sun-on-his-back.

So there is something universal about this, which suggests it has its roots in psychology as much as in history. Long after the Brits had got the hell out of these countries, England was still fulfilling this role of the cartoon baddie, the hated father figure, the ogre in whose demise we take great delight, mocking him as he is undone yet again by the little guy.

And the old football hooliganism wasn't doing them any favours either.

So everyone had an axe to grind with Johnny England, though in our case, there may even be a benign interpretation. It was perhaps our way of taking the heat out of the conflict, of reducing it from a war to something more like a pantomime. Because of course there was still a war going on, although the 'armed struggle' had become so obviously pointless and grotesque, most Irish people were moving away from it anyway, and would not be coming back.

The young Irish in London in the late 1980s were discovering other ways of keeping in touch with their roots, not least by following The Pogues, who were putting together an inspirational body of work which would re-define Irish musical culture and make it better. You could never listen to the Wolfe Tones again after hearing *Rum, Sodomy & the Lash* — yes, in the spirit of the times, it seemed right for that magical album to borrow its title from a line of Churchill's.

The enthusiasm with which we still celebrated these great England defeats may be seen in the context of an end to the war, rather than its perpetuation. After all that had happened, it would probably have been unnatural just to 'draw a line under it', as they say, and to 'move on', and behave like perfect gentlemen. So now we were turning it into a form of entertainment, knowing that there would be an almost endless supply of material, not just from the England football team, but from the accompanying circus of TV commentators and patriotic pundits such as Jimmy Hill and horrible tabloid hacks, monstering their own boys for our delectation.

And there was something deeply funny about the England team of that era, from any perspective. England was always expecting something that just couldn't be delivered and wouldn't be delivered, resulting in a succession of pratfalls which were increasingly hilarious for the 'neutrals'. For the English themselves, their apparently endless suffering since 1966 and their inability to manage these great expectations had broken them down to such an extent, it had degenerated into something that was manic and hysterical and ultimately quite barking. In fact, their poor manager Bobby Robson would be maddened in every sense of the word during Euro 88 and the Italia 90 campaign which was still ahead of him.

That would be the same Sir Bobby who eventually became the supremo of ... the Republic of Ireland. Which tells us that either he had forgiven us or we had forgiven him. Or that there wasn't much badness in it, in the first place.

We had had our fun and eventually, we really were ready to move on.

———

On the morning after Ireland's victory in Stuttgart I arrived back in Heathrow having flown through the night from New York — the plane was delayed for hours in JFK, leaving me with no alternative but to begin the celebrations on the ground with a few more cold beers, then show what seemed to me like admirable restraint in the air — while I smoked a few hundred cigarettes as usual I don't recall being very, very drunk, but then there was such a strange combination of sensations going on: the lack of sleep, the defeat of England, and the beer already on board, I was probably experiencing some disorder of the senses that I had never gone through before.

I do recall being merry enough to indulge in a bit of banter with a newspaper vendor at Heathrow about what Paddy had done to him the previous day. But he didn't want to play.

It seemed to be of vital importance to read as many English papers as possible, to savour their shame and their savagery towards their own boys. So while I waited for the flight back to Dublin, I devoured them all, broadsheet and tabloid. Christ, it was fine stuff. The prevailing theme was that England had not just lost disgracefully, they had lost to a team which was generally characterised as a rag-bag of plodders and journeymen, thrown together by Big Jack in the course of some desperate trawl through the lower regions of the English leagues.

And Packie Bonner, who played in Scotland, was largely a stranger to them, too, just some geezer who would be going back to the obscurity from whence he came, but who had played like the devil himself, the way that the crazed keeper Tomascevski had played for Poland on another night of sin, a long time ago.

Had they any idea how much we were enjoying this? Evidently not, but then they didn't really care about us. They were just using our supposed awfulness as yet another weapon with which to batter Bobby Robson and his pampered superstars such as Kenny Sansom, Gary Stevens and Neil Webb. They had Loadsamoney and we had none, but what good was it to them?

By now Christy Moore would be finishing off the writing of his new ballad, 'Joxer Goes To Stuttgart', and the story was still unfolding. We would face the Soviet Union on Wednesday and Holland the following Saturday. But we did not want to step out of this England reverie yet. We would still have a couple of days to get ourselves up for the Soviets and what Jack called 'Wor Dutch', and we had no idea if the lads could get it up again for those challenges.

Let us not forget that there were only eight teams in this Euro 88, that there was a heightened sense of belonging to an elite, or at least belonging to a group which contained an elite. There was nowhere to turn in that competition without encountering some deeply intimidating prospect, some potential trauma of epochal proportions.

But since the most terrifying one had passed, what was the worst that could happen to us now? That we would get turned over by the Russians or Wor Dutch? Well, there could be some suffering on the way there, as it was now becoming clear to me, with the papers read, that England had been all over us to such an extent that most men who had lived through it would never be the same again.

Soon I would be hearing of men drinking savagely all the way through that match, drinking whiskey straight from the bottle, beseeching the gods to stop the pain. If Gary Lineker and John Barnes could do that to us, what could Ruud Gullit and Marco Van Basten do?

So rarefied was this competition, that even after winning the first match, we might still not even qualify from the group. After all our hard work breaking the hearts of the English, would it make no difference in the end on the old scoreboard? After all that, would we be flying home from Germany on the same day as those poor unfortunate men?

Right now we could live with that. We had not entirely lost sight of the facts of football life, so we knew that we just weren't as good as Wor Dutch, that we mightn't be quite on the same page as the Russians, who had actually beaten Wor Dutch 1-0, and after what England had done to us, and what we had gotten away with, we wondered in quiet moments if we were any good at all — for Paddy, even as he received the love and the admiration of a grateful world, the old demons would still be gnawing away at him.

One recalled a moment of spontaneous hilarity at Lansdowne during the match against Bulgaria in the qualifiers, when Mick McCarthy had embarked on something of an unlikely solo run and a shout had gone up from the stand, 'Show them your class, Mick!'

And it wasn't just the crowd that laughed. Mick himself no doubt saw the funny side of it, the truth in it.

Ah, yes, at some deep level, we knew our place.

And then as the Republic duly went up against the Soviet Union (or 'the might of the Soviet Union' to give them their full title) the strangest thing of all happened.

We got good.

That night in Hanover will always be encapsulated in the image of McCarthy's long throw-in to Ronnie Whelan and Ronnie's volley to the top corner of the net, and his fist-pumping celebration.

For Jack it would have been almost the perfect goal, virtually no fannying around at any point of the proceedings, though if Mick had managed to throw it straight into the net, with maybe a tiny deflection to make it legal, all the better.

Yet the effort from Ronnie was glorious, reminding us that no-one ever laughed when Ronnie went on a solo run, no-one ever shouted 'Show them your class!' Ronnie was all class, a first-rate player with the best club side in the world, one of those awkward little facts which upset the preferred tabloid narrative of the rag-bag of plodders and journeymen.

Liam Brady would have added to the confusion except he had been injured in the run-up to Euro 88 and would probably not have made it anyway due to a suspension for a red card against Bulgaria.

Jack would later say that he was delighted with Liam in that match, that 'the penny had finally dropped with Liam', that Liam had now put aside all that shit he used to do for Juventus, and was playing as Jack wanted him to play, taking the ball from the front players, rather than taking it from the defence and building it from there. And generally fannying around. But even though Liam had seen the light, it was generally felt that Jack wasn't entirely gutted when Liam couldn't make it, after all he had contributed to the cause, and the things that he had seen.

And this performance against the Soviet Union would crystallise a conflict which would grow deeper as time went by.

We were now starting to accept that we had always had these players of the highest class, but that Jack had forged them into a unit that could compete and win and not be afraid of anyone. But in doing that, perhaps he would deny them the freedom to move to a higher level, maybe even to play like Wor Dutch, who had never made any distinction between the desire to play good football and the desire to win, who believed, in fact, that you couldn't have one without the other and who had been vindicated in this belief, many times.

The Republic played good football against the Soviet Union that night. But we didn't win. Yes, we were good, but they still equalised with a soft goal with fifteen minutes to go. And we should have had a penalty when Galvin was fouled by the fabled keeper Dasayev.

For a moment there, we were back in hell again, back in the days when Stapleton would be scoring against France and against Belgium, and having it ruled out for no reason. Back in the days of Brussels in the pouring rain and Bulgarian prostitutes.

But God, we were good that night in Hanover. And why wouldn't we be good, with Ronnie on the park and Kevin Sheedy and Chris Hughton and Tony Galvin, and Aldo knocking them in, or not, as the case may be? Houghton could play a bit, and Kevin Moran would not be found wanting in any situation, in sport or in life itself.

This indeed, was becoming apparent, too, about the Boys In Green — they were not just good, they were also 'good lads', as the football man would have it. They were generally bright guys, they had a bit of character, they gave the impression they had not been created in some test-tube in a football laboratory, but that they had lived a bit — in the case of Big Paul, maybe they had lived a bit too much. Which still didn't stop him making an enormous contribution.

Paul had a header cleared off the line in the group decider against Wor Dutch in Gelsenkirchen. And he played in midfield, as distinct from the centre-half role in which he would appear to be playing the opposition entirely on his own, anticipating everything and stopping it without ever apparently feeling the need to fall back on the more old-fashioned football tricks, such as running.

But the Republic on the whole were not good that day, and Wor Dutch were not much better. I watched it at home in the flat in Dun Laoghaire on a small television — I would never watch a match on such a small television again. My friend George Byrne had gone to Germany, and he would recall sitting outside the ground after the match, being consoled by a Dutch couple. Again and again the crazy ricochet from Kieft which sent the ball looping and spinning past Packie, kept running in his head, along with this tormenting mantra: 'Seven minutes … seven minutes …' Mercifully he was unaware that the baleful gods had thrown in another sickener, what with Van Basten being in an offside position and unquestionably interfering with play, for Kieft's ridiculous goal.

And it was actually more like nine minutes still to go, or, if you like, 'Teenage Kicks' played three times in a row. Except this time it seemed to be playing at 78 rpm.

———

That Dutch couple found it easy to empathise with George — after all, they had seen a couple of World Cup Finals slipping away, one of them in Germany itself, playing football of such mesmerising beauty even now the thought of it stirs the blood. But this was our first taste of losing at this level, of seeing some ludicrously large prize just out of reach, a place in the semi-final denied us by these aristocrats who would duly go on to win the tournament. And we wondered if indeed we had any right to be knocking the likes of them out of the tournament, as we would have done if we had held out for the draw.

They would play the Soviet Union in the Final. That would be the same Soviet Union that we had 'beaten' 1-1.

Holland would win Euro 88, by which stage we would be just enjoying the weather. I have no idea what the weather was actually like during those weeks. But in the mind's eye, the sky was blue and the sun shone all the time.

Chapter 5 ∽

SOMETIMES YOU JUST CAN'T MAKE IT ON YOUR OWN

The Homecoming gave us not just another day out but one of the enduring lines of the Charlton years. Somewhere in the centre of Dublin City, from the top of the bus, an elated Ray Houghton started up the chant: 'Who put the ball in the England net?'

If there had been any question at all that Houghton was one of our own, this settled it. He was Paddy, to the core. And he also seemed instinctively to understand that while he was obviously having his fun at the expense of the country which had provided him with an exceptionally good living and all the opportunities he needed to become Paddy in the first place, it was also just that — it was just fun.

A few months previously, at Milltown cemetery in Belfast, the loyalist Michael Stone had materialised at the grave of three IRA members shot dead while on active service in Gibraltar by the SAS. In a scene which was filmed as it happened by the television cameras, Stone fired several shots and threw grenades, and could then be seen shooting at his pursuers as he ran from the cemetery. He had killed three people and injured 60, bringing a macabre new dimension to the North, where until that day, it was generally accepted that the one safe place was the graveyard.

And then at the funeral of one of Stone's victims, two plain-clothes British army corporals, who were observing the proceedings in an unmarked car, were spotted by republican mourners. Their car was surrounded by a frenzied mob, some of whom would later claim that they feared another Stone-like attack. The two Brits were dragged from the car and beaten and shot to death. Pictures of their naked bodies lying on waste land were seen all over the world.

Now, at the height of summer, Ray Houghton could be heard singing 'Who put the ball in the England net?' to the tune of 'The Camptown Races', and it came across like a regular line of sporting banter. The sort of line you'd hear in the context of some ancient and intense sporting rivalry between, say, Kerry and Dublin. Ancient and intense, but perhaps not quite as violent as the rivalry between Kerry and Dublin.

So it seemed as if the football team had carved out a territory in which we might have a normal level of hostility with our neighbours, played out in a sporting manner, the way that normal countries do. It seemed as if the Englishness of Charlton and about half his team had helped to make that possible by demonstrating that there were just too many links between Ireland and England to sustain the idea that we were implacable enemies.

And that those links were tending to redound to our benefit, rather than theirs.

Maybe it's just the potency of football, the deep importance of it, that helped to convey this impression that something unique was going on here in the context of Anglo-Irish relations and of our relationship with the rest of the world. But if we really take a look at ourselves, we can see that the emergence of the football team was just the most compelling example of a phenomenon which had been happening in an understated way for a very long time.

It's not entirely true to say that Paddy just can't make it on his own, but it is certainly true to say that Paddy generally does a lot better when he mixes it up a bit, when he fuses his own talents with the talents of others.

And it goes well beyond the 'great-grandmother' rule and the diaspora.

It even goes beyond the human, when you consider that the world's greatest trainer of racehorses, Vincent O'Brien, sought the best of American bloodstock. And to get them across the line he had the greatest of all English jockeys, Lester Piggott.

In so many fields, for a very long time, we have been quietly availing of the services of those who do not belong to our gene-pool, who were not born in Ireland, but who have been an intrinsic part of almost every 'Irish' cultural project which has been internationally successful. Starting with the most bleeding obvious example, two of the members of U2 are not Irish in the straightforward sense of being born in Ireland or having Irish parents: the Edge's people are from Wales, and he was born in England, as was Adam Clayton. And Bono's mother came from the Protestant tradition, which is more a part of our English than our Irish heritage. Their mentor, Bill Graham, was from the North. Or, if you like, the United Kingdom. And their manager, Paul McGuinness, was born in Germany.

The film *My Left Foot* was universally regarded as an all-Irish international success, and of course director Jim Sheridan and producer Noel Pearson are Irish to all intents and purposes, yet one of the Oscars was won by Daniel Day-Lewis, who is in many ways, deeply English. Due to his complex bohemian background, he is also deeply Irish in many ways, but again, there's a mixture here. Would a conventionally Irish actor, born and reared in this country, have delivered such an extraordinary performance? Maybe he would have done. We will never know.

But Neil Jordan surely, is Irish in every way? Yes, but much of his most successful work has been done in collaboration with the producer Stephen Woolley, who is English. They would appear to understand each other at a creative level. And Jordan would also acknowledge a debt to his mentor in film-making, John Boorman, who has lived in Ireland for many years but who is definitely English.

It is an interdependence and a source of mutual inspiration that was perhaps most powerfully seen in the relationship between Brian Keenan and John McCarthy, the Irishman and the Englishman who were in captivity in Beirut at this time. They would be released in 1990 and 1991 respectively, having completely missed Euro 88 and Italia 90 and their friendship would be viewed as a rare example of the Irish and the English coming together in a common cause.

But as we are seeing, it is not so rare after all.

We have already alluded to this potent fusion in the area of rock 'n' roll, whereby the children of Irish emigrants would be regarded as Paddies by the English and as Brits by their relations back in Ireland, in Roscommon and Cork and Mayo where they would go for their summer holidays. They were mixed-race in a way that seemed to lead to enormous creativity. Enormous pain, no doubt, in many ways, too, but pain that produced Johnny Rotten and Morrissey and the Gallaghers and Shane MacGowan.

The Pogues were actually derided early doors by the traditional musician Noel Hill, for what they were doing to Irish music. But while the purists felt they were bringing us into disrepute with their noise and their drinking, the rest of the world could see that a beautiful thing was happening here with this London-Irish combo. They had created this sound of the Irish in England which you felt had somehow always existed, just waiting to be released — but not by the Irish acting alone. In this context the narrow nationalism of Sinn Féin, 'ourselves alone', can be seen to have brought us not just a thousand pointless murders, but was Paddy's sure-fire recipe for failure.

Roddy Doyle may have fulfilled all the criteria for full-blown Irishness, but his commercial success was assisted by the brilliance of Alan Parker's version of *The Commitments*, which was made with American money and which turned Roddy's slim debut novel into a barnstorming modern musical — that would be the same Alan Parker, who was so disappointed to hear us cheering the misfortunes of his England team as he scouted for locations in Dublin pubs. And then there were the film versions of *The Snapper* and *The Van*, superbly directed by Stephen Frears, an Englishman, of course. Roddy, indeed, would be an obvious collaborator with the English, because English football is his game, and the game of his male characters. They speak of doing things 'the Liverpool way', as naturally as their Gaelic literary forbears spoke of getting the pikes together at the rising of the moon.

I am thinking also of Arthur Mathews, Graham Linehan, Dermot Morgan, Ardal O'Hanlon and Pauline McLynn who were all football men and women — all, at least, apart from Graham. Whilst they could put together one of the most successful comedy series of all time, featuring situations and characters who were quintessentially Irish, again they could only do it with the generous support of the English, such as the late Geoffrey Perkins, a producer who believed in them. (You can still find people who think that Ireland's indigenous TV service RTÉ turned down *Father Ted*, but the truth is actually worse than that — RTÉ never got the chance to turn it down, because it never occurred to the lads to offer it to them in the first place.)

In fairness to us, we have always openly acknowledged the Anglo-Irishness of some of our most celebrated writers, of Yeats and Synge and Beckett. We have never denied that Wilde and Shaw and Goldsmith and Richard Brinsley Sheridan needed to join forces with all sorts of English types to make their genius known, or that Sean O'Casey — who, like Bono, is from the Protestant tradition — eventually preferred to live and work among the English. There was Joyce, who might appear like a rare exception to the rule, until you recall that he may have been all Irish himself, but he found it necessary to get out of here, in a hurry, in order to be discovered by the cognoscenti of Paris. And of course, the hero of *Ulysses*, the definitive Irish epic, was the Jewish Leopold Bloom. Not exactly your card-carrying, bona-fide, full-metal-jacket Paddy there.

Nor were Micheál MacLiammóir and Hilton Edwards, founders of the Gate theatre, who constructed this weird and marvellous façade of Irishness around themselves, perhaps to take our minds off the fact that they weren't Irish at all, but English.

You might be thinking though, that Christy Moore is Irish, in every possible way and that is true. But then Christy is not universally known and internationally successful in the sense of having hit records in Britain and America and all around the world. Not like Chris de Burgh, for example, whose father was British and who lived in Argentina as a child.

Brendan Behan himself, whose image would appear on any tea-towel featuring the faces of Ireland's most celebrated writers, is an interesting case. Behan's sensibility was largely influenced by two things — his membership of the IRA, which involved him in the bombing campaign in England for which he was sent to borstal, and the borstal itself, which broadened his view of life and gave him the material for his best work, *Borstal Boy*.

You could compare this awakening to the way a raw young Irish footballer would go to England with a lot of ability but a lot of bad habits too, which would be knocked out of him in one of the great ball-playing institutions of Manchester or Liverpool. All of which, in the fullness of time, would leave him better prepared to serve his own country, in a more constructive fashion.

It is also universally acknowledged that Behan's work in the theatre was championed and largely shaped by Joan Littlewood, who was born in Stockwell, a part of London not unknown to Paddy in the 1980s. The young Conor McPherson was similarly nurtured by the Bush Theatre in London and Martin McDonagh, lest we forget, is a Londoner by birth.

Behan himself, who kept a close watch on the Paddy in all of us, would have noted the ironies and paradoxes of his revolutionary roots, the fact that the men of 1916 included Pádraig Pearse, whose father was from Birmingham and would not have qualified to play football for Ireland, and James Connolly who was Scottish and who could only have played for the Republic that he envisioned under the parentage rule. When you add in exotics such as Roger Casement to the mixer, you can see that even in the defining narrative of Irish independence, Paddy couldn't quite make it on his own.

Dana herself is from Northern Ireland, which is another country. Jesus H. Christ, even Foster & Allen, who gave us a few anxious moments with those kilts they were sporting on *Top Of the Pops*, were singing 'A Bunch Of Thyme', which is thought to be of English origin.

The search for the 'true' Irish goes on: Bob Geldof's people are originally from Belgium; Sinead O'Connor's great hit was written by a little guy from Minneapolis called Prince Rogers Nelson; Phil Lynott, being black, would not exactly be viewed as the stereotypical Irishman and rightly so, as he was born in Birmingham and his father was from Brazil, but his statue now stands in Harry Street, just off Grafton Street, where Glen Hansard of The Frames used to do his busking; Glen, who somehow won the Oscar for best song, when the no-budget Irish movie *Once* miraculously became an international hit. Which might seem like an extremely rare all-Irish success story until you remember that the song 'Falling Slowly' was co-written by Hansard's co-star in the film, Markéta Irglová, who is from the Czech Republic — a new stop there on the traditional route.

No doubt I'm forgetting a few things here, but I don't think I'm forgetting much — Seamus Heaney became very successful in the late 1980s but again we tend to forget that Seamus is from Northern Ireland, which is part of the United Kingdom. He would have played his football not for the Republic, but for Norn Iron.

All of which leaves us with … Enya. Yes, Enya is entirely Irish, every day, in every way. And so is her music. Except, now that I think of it, Enya's recordings are essentially a collaboration with her producers, Nicky Ryan and his wife Roma, who writes the lyrics. And Roma is from Belfast, which is in Northern Ireland, which again we must remind ourselves, is part of the United Kingdom. So Enya doesn't count either, in our quest to find something that is purely Irish and in no way English or American or Belgian or Brazilian but especially English — and that is internationally successful. To which the 'wags' might respond that the Boys In Green themselves have no place in this discussion, because they never won anything, or came close to winning anything.

But we will ignore that gibe, for the moment.

In terms of a victory on the international stage that was down to Paddy and nobody but Paddy in the purest sense, that we could truly say was ours and ours alone, to the best of my recollection there is … the Eurovision Song Contest. In fact, there would eventually be seven Eurovisions. But wait … There's no way around this …

Johnny Logan was born in Australia.

Chapter 6 ∿

THIS WAS NOT A
FOOTBALL MATCH

The breakthrough, I believe, was against Spain. As we look back on those years, we tend to see it all as one extended breakthrough. But there were breakthroughs within the greater breakthrough. And the greatest of these was at Lansdowne Road against Spain on 26 April 1989, in the qualifying campaign for Italia 90. It was a game against a great football nation that we absolutely had to win and that we actually won — it had never happened before in the Charlton era (we didn't absolutely have to beat England in Stuttgart) and it would never happen again (Romania is not a great football nation and while we would beat them on penalties in the last 16 of Italia 90, the match itself was a scoreless draw).

After the fine madness of Euro 88 we had been re-connected to reality in the first match of the new campaign, receiving a right royal rogering from Johnny Spaniard in Seville the previous November. The result was 2-0, but it felt a lot worse than that. It felt just like old times, in fact, to be playing against these guys who were bred in the purple and to have our lack of class so clearly exposed.

Reduced to the simplest terms, such encounters tended to demonstrate that those guys were just much better at football than our guys. Anyone who has ever played football can relate to that at a visceral level. It brings you back to the schoolyard to an under-12 match, where it is plain to see that some lads are just better than others, they have more talent. You might keep them out for a while, these lads who are just better at football, by dint of hard work and honesty of effort and the vague hope that they don't really give a damn anyway. But they'll get you in the end.

And though you've tried so hard, maybe in the end it's not that hard to accept. Because it is, after all, the truth.

So the slaughter in Seville, at one level, felt a bit like nature taking its course. We could live with that, as we have always lived with it. And maybe we felt we needed to be reminded of the eternal verities, to submit ourselves to the tyranny of fact.

At Euro 88, we had played three, won one, drawn one and lost one.

We had not qualified from the group. It was a breakthrough just to be able to compete, but there was another breakthrough which had eluded us. Perhaps because, for all our undoubted charms, we just weren't good enough at football.

Yes, we had beaten England, but they had battered us, and on another day they would have scored. Yes, we had played something that looked remarkably like football against the USSR, but high on the improbability of it all, we hadn't got the result. And they, with their innate Soviet know-how and cunning, had qualified. Not us. And while that late goal in Gelsenkirchen had made us curse the baleful gods, it hadn't fooled us into thinking that we were actually as good as Holland, either on that day, or on any other day.

So we were in a new place in the aftermath of Euro 88, an exciting place but a dangerous place nonetheless for Paddy.

Having established that everyone liked us, was it possible that they might also come to respect us?

———

It is one of our great character defects, this desperate desire to be liked.

'What do you think of us?', we openly ask, when foreigners come to Ireland, and they seem to understand that we don't really want an honest answer. We don't really want them to provide us with a detailed assessment of our good points and our bad points, we just want them to say, 'You're great'.

Which they usually do, the way that you'd humour a child. We know they're only telling us what we want to hear, but we don't mind that. And we don't exactly respect ourselves for this, but then we are not asking to be respected. We are only asking to be liked.

At Euro 88, we had been liked. At least we assumed we had been liked and very well liked, because we had done everything in our power to achieve this happy state. We had behaved ourselves so well, we had brought scenes of great joy to the terraces, with our green wigs and our bodhráns and our gas characters; we had been able to hold our drink.

At least that's how we saw it, so we trusted that's how everyone else saw it. Certainly a few English broadsheets weighed in with their usual generosity towards us and their loathing of their own kind, the hooligans who can't behave themselves like good old Paddy.

So there was some sort of official confirmation that we had been liked. So great was our need in this regard, we found it hard to imagine that the citizens of other countries might have gone through that tournament without thinking much about Paddy at all — that they might indeed go through their entire lives without thinking about the Irish, let alone forming a view as to our likeability, until they are asked a direct question — do you like us? — to which there can only be the one answer.

There would be a particularly poignant example of this acute self-consciousness towards the end of the Charlton years, when we had qualified for the 1994 World Cup and there was much speculation about the possible venues for the Republic's matches. It was widely suggested by well-respected commentators (well-liked at any rate) that the Irish were so popular all around the world, and especially in America, that they were bound to end up playing in one of the great Irish-American cities such as Chicago or Boston.

Essentially, it was being proposed that FIFA, the football's world governing body, would rig the draw for our benefit because we're such great fellows and they like us so much. In our imagination, we could see the top brass of FIFA addressing this matter of over-whelming importance, discussing at length how best to arrange the tournament so that Paddy gets all that Irish-American support. We were 'the best supporters in the world', after all, so it wasn't just that they liked us — that was a given — hell, they needed us.

So it was utterly inexplicable, and bordering on the perverse, to discover that we were just thrown into the draw along with all the other countries, and that we would be forced to play in frigging Orlando, in the blazing heat, against Mexico. You would almost think that we were just another team, that we were not the most-liked. And as for respect, you would have more respect for a dog than to be dragging him from New York to Orlando and back again — yes, the Irish did get to play in New York, in front of their own people, but that could also be construed as a gift to the Italians, so it didn't count. It was down to the hot-house of Orlando and back again to New York for the third match against Norway.

You would hardly wish such a thing on someone you hated, let alone on the best supporters in the world.

Mind you, we would have gratefully accepted all these perceived slights, and a lot more, after the slaughter in Seville back at the end of 1988.

To maintain at least some of the morale that we had gained in Germany, we could reflect on the undoubted fact that in Seville, we had been without four very important players — Houghton, Sheedy, Whelan and McGrath.

We had also given Steve Staunton his first cap, with Kevin Moran in front of him in midfield and David O'Leary beside him at centre-half — yes, Jack was desperate enough on the night, to play O'Leary — all these things, by any standard, constituted a perfectly valid excuse.

So we still had hope.

But that, too, is a dangerous place for Paddy. We have sat looking into enough glasses of whiskey to know that hope is never too far away from ruin, in the order of things. Hope and ruin, the old reliables.

Indeed the fact that the group also contained Northern Ireland seemed to exacerbate this sense that everything was still in the balance, that it could all go either way. We had no consciousness of anything but bad things emanating from our relationship with Northern Ireland and we assumed that this would be no different.

Appropriately, after three games in the group, we had only two points, one of them garnered against Norn Iron in a match in Windsor Park which most of us have forgotten entirely — every aspect of it, down to the last detail, has been entirely expunged from our memories.

Most people to whom I have spoken still have vivid and horrendous recollections of the match in Windsor Park in 1993 which sent the Republic to the 1994 World Cup, but in the case of the scoreless draw back in 1988, when there was still a war going on, denial set in almost immediately, leading quickly to total amnesia.

There was also a scoreless draw with Hungary, in Budapest, in March 1989, which again raised the issue of our self-esteem. Because despite having supped the fine wine of Euro 88, we could not see ourselves as the sort of people who might be disappointed with one point instead of three. After all, Hungary, as the Mighty Magyars back in the 1950s, had featured in one of the Ten Great England Defeats. So we would naturally have a healthy respect for them.

Or perhaps an unhealthy respect: for sure, they weren't the Mighty Magyars any more, but from where we were looking, they still looked mighty enough.

Hungary was the first international team I ever saw in the flesh, playing at Dalymount on a Sunday afternoon back in the late 1960s. I recall that the stars of Hungarian football at that time were Ferenc Bene and Florian Albert, who exuded class, and that they won with a late goal, as was only to be expected. In general, they seemed to be much, much better at football than we were.

My memories of such matches are clouded by the fact that I never saw Ireland scoring a goal. When it looked like they might score, everyone would stand up, mad with anticipation and since I was only a child, my view would be entirely blocked. I could only listen, either for the orgasmic roar or the sigh of disappointment. So I never saw Ireland scoring a goal, but I heard them scoring a few.

Never enough, it seemed.

Twenty years later, even against a football nation which was clearly in decline, a draw in Hungary would seem reasonable — after all, they were in decline from such heights and we were rising from such depths, maybe we were just meeting them in the middle.

It was also somewhat troubling that we had scored no goals in the first three matches of the group, though this could also be rationalised — we had been away from home, against a very good team, a useful enough team, and Northern Ireland.

And having played the first three games away, even if we hadn't been impressive, we were still alive. Normally, at this stage, we would have expected to be dead.

So there was a sense that the worst was over us, if you discount the lingering spectre of Northern Ireland still waiting for us in the last match of the group — ah, we had many, many miles to go, on this journey.

Even the idea of playing the first three matches away from home was a new concept for us, hopefully another example of Jack's original thinking, which would yield the same success as his most original thinking of all, which was to play football without actually playing football as such. At least, not as anyone else was playing it in the civilised world.

We were still not free of this ingrained sense of foreboding, even though we could finish second in the Group and still qualify automatically.

Assuming that Spain would win the Group and Northern Ireland would get beaten often enough to do them down and Malta would get beaten by everyone, it was effectively between ourselves and Hungary, the not-so-mighty Magyars.

Not the most awe-inspiring task.

Still we feared the worst.

Still we feared ruin.

It takes more than just a few good football results to get over that ancient feeling, so we feared all the things we have always feared, until the day that Spain came to Lansdowne.

I went to that match with George Byrne, the controversial rock journalist. We would later see deep significance in the fact that the last match we had attended together was the final agony of the Eoin Hand era, a famously wretched 4-1 defeat at home to Denmark in 1985. And we had even missed seeing the Republic's goal. We were only arriving into the stand at the moment that Frank Stapleton headed the first goal of the match, early doors.

The rest would be a débâcle, with the stadium full of mad Danes wearing Viking helmets with horns celebrating the best team they would ever have, bound for the 1986 World Cup in Mexico while we looked on forlornly, excluded from life's banquet.

It was but a small consolation that we hadn't paid in to that match, because I had been given two free tickets by the PR company putting together the match programme, who used an article of mine from *Hot Press*, a piece in the Foul Play column on the fabled RTÉ football commentator Philip Greene. They also gave me £25, as I recall, along with the two tickets, and we were undoubtedly drinking that money in the International Bar later that evening when the well-known folklorist and professional Dubliner Éamonn MacThomáis walked in and declared in his usual heart-of-the-rowel style, 'Ah, Brian Boru was the only fella who could beat them Danes!'

At that moment, we knew we were in hell, that we were at the point known to alcoholics as rock bottom — and still we had a lot of drinking to do on that night and in the nights to come.

———

So it seemed meaningful that four years later, in April 1989, George and I were marching on Lansdowne in a much different frame of mind. It might be a portent of the worst kind, our presence ensuring some similarly nightmarish outcome, or it might be a good omen, a reward for all we had suffered in the days when the likes of us were the only people still following the Republic — and we were getting in free, with our beer money thrown in.

Was it too much to expect that on this day, against Spain who had butchered us in Seville, there might be something akin to what the psycho-babblers call 'closure'?

On the whole, Paddy doesn't do closure. But we came very close to it, on the day we beat Spain 1-0 at Lansdowne. You could hardly even call it a football match, this exhibition of barely-controlled savagery on the part of the Republic. And the Spaniards wouldn't call it a football match either: 'This was not a football match, it was not even close', their striker, Emilio Butragueno, known as The Vulture, would later protest. 'The Irish players were too harsh.'

And he hadn't mentioned the crowd, who themselves had been a tad harsh.

There were about 50,000 in Lansdowne that day because thousands could still stand at matches, pressed up against the wire, screaming at Johnny Spaniard. It was just a few weeks after the Hillsborough Disaster. Soon, there would be no more of this standing at Lansdowne Road or at any other football ground.

Not that Lansdowne was a football ground, in truth. For the visit of Johnny Spaniard, with all his poise and his superb technique, Lansdowne was a rugby pitch. It was so rough, no-one could have played football on it, even if they tried. Not even Johnny Spaniard. 'It was very difficult to play in these circumstances', The Vulture remarked, apparently not fully aware that this was precisely the idea and that Jack had been known to compliment the groundsman on his performance on such days.

I was close to the wire that day and I could see that The Vulture and his illustrious colleagues were struggling. Whenever a Spaniard came to take a throw-in he would be horribly abused by the mob behind the wire, a mob which was starting to get the smell of fear from their refined visitors and another smell which was driving them on to greater obscenities — the smell of victory.

Ireland scored after 17 minutes.

It turned out to be an own-goal by the celebrated Michel, from a cross by Houghton. Another kind break there, for Jack, who even lucked in to the correct pronunciation of the Spaniard's name in the post-match press conference. 'Mitchell' he called him, to the guffaws of the reporters who assumed in their cosmopolitan way that it must be pronounced 'Michelle'. It turned out that 'Mitchell' was right.

During the game some of us thought that Stapleton had scored it, a sweet irony for myself and George, though in effect we didn't see this one either, our view blocked by the crowd heaving all around us. In fact Stapo scoring would have been somewhat problematic for

Jack himself, who seemed to be making it his business to liquidate Paddy's heroes of old, such as Brady and O'Leary and Stapleton, perhaps to show Paddy who was in charge, perhaps because he genuinely hated the football they played.

So Stapleton was still giving Jack a pain in the arse but he had his uses. Which is more than could be said for The Vulture, the predator who was supposed to devour us, but who was himself taken off during the second-half, sending the crowd into a new level of frenzy. I can still feel the animalistic energy of that day, that heightened sense that if we won this match, we were going to a better place, for a long time, and if we couldn't win it, we were utterly screwed, for a long time. A sense that all we had gained in the madness of Euro 88 was now on the line.

I remember Staunton in particular because he was on our side of the pitch. In these all-seater days, you get a proper perspective on the match, but in the last days of the old regime, from where we were standing, it seemed to be all about Staunton, stopping everything that came his way, charging and chasing and harassing.

For a lot of the folks on those terraces, this was the defining match of the Charlton years, and nothing would be quite the same again. The multitudes with their Olé Olé-ing and their que-sera-sera-ing would now be signing themselves up for full membership of a club to which they had never really belonged and which they would never rightly understand.

Football itself would never be the same again — in fact John Aldridge wasn't playing against Spain because he was still traumatised after Hillsborough.

And just as football seemed to be dying in its ancient heartlands, for Ireland, football seemed to be promising the world.

There was a routine 2-0 home win against Malta (ah, how blithely we dismiss these little people). Though even then, I recall writing a piece in the *Sunday Independent* which mentioned a thing called

PMT, or 'pre-Maltese tension'. We got over that, and on a sunny Sunday in June 1989, there was an extraordinarily happy day for Ireland when we beat Hungary 2-0, a game distinguished by a particularly fine opening goal from Paul McGrath. Even Paddy, with all his perfectly justified fatalism, was starting to believe that he was about to qualify for the World Cup for the first time.

I watched that one from the Press Box, perhaps feeling that I wasn't needed any more, down in the pit — and soon, there wouldn't even be a pit.

In fact as the Group progressed, my viewing arrangements seemed to reflect the broader trends. Having stood with the howling mob against Spain, I then found myself in the relative serenity of the main stand for the Hungary match. For the home match against Northern Ireland, a 3-0 win which was realised almost contemptuously after a nervous first half, I had moved my operation to the Purty Loft in Dun Laoghaire, drinking pints of lager all day and watching it on a big screen. And for the ceremonial defeat of Malta in their Ta' Qali stadium, I had moved to an even bigger screen in a banqueting room in Sachs Hotel, where *Hot Press* had organised a party, attended by various rock personalities, most notably Mr Joe Elliott of Def Leppard. Though I should add that Joe was not just some celebrity cheering all the wrong things at the wrong time, but a football man of impeccable pedigree, a fiercely committed Sheffield Utd fan — and like most Englishmen, he wished us well.

Hot Press, too, was entitled to have a bit of a do, in view of its outstanding loyalty to the game in this country, exemplified by the Foul Play column and the growing reputation on the field of play of the grand old club *Hot Press* Moenchengladbach. The fact that a party was being thrown with the result not absolutely one hundred per cent certain tells its own story of the breakthroughs we were all making.

But the gods were still throwing odd little barriers in the way of our pursuit of happiness.

Fog descended on Dublin Airport in the days before the match, with fans becoming increasingly anxious that they might not get off the island in time. And anxiety naturally leads to the consumption of alcohol in very large quantities — especially if you're hanging around an airport for a long time and you're wearing a green, white and gold curly wig and your name is Paddy. Happiness also has that effect, as does sadness and all the hobgoblins to which we are prey. But this time it was the anxiety that was sucking up the booze.

On RTÉ News, as the crisis deepened, a woman was seen weeping bitterly.

Having had their sport with us, those baleful gods lifted the fog on Wednesday morning, allowing just enough time for everyone to get out there and to see us beating Malta 2-0. Even if some of them only got there for the second half, Paddy would, after all, have his day in the sun.

Beyond in Malta, at the Ta' Qali National Stadium in Valletta, the gentlemen of the press would be filing their triumphalist reports, perhaps recalling a less happy time, when one of their number was not so sure of the outcome.

He had been one of several journalists who had partaken of a long and leisurely lunch on the day that the Republic were playing Malta in a European Championship qualifier. Perhaps the local wine was fortified, because this particular reporter seemed to be still feeling the effects later that evening, during and after the match — his colleagues heard him muttering angrily on the bus back to the hotel, that it was a disgrace that Ireland had sunk so low they couldn't even beat these eejits from Malta. Yet they had beaten Malta, albeit narrowly, with a late goal from Stapleton, which had apparently gone unnoticed by the reporter.

As his colleagues manoeuvred him back to his room, they feared for him. When they had lashed out their own reports in their own rooms, a few of his colleagues went to this man's room to check on his condition.

They knocked on his door, but there was no answer. They tried to enter the room, but it was locked. So with the help of a concierge with the master key they entered his room, which was now in darkness.

Through the gloom, they could see a figure sitting at a table, apparently fast asleep, slumped over a typewriter. Instantly they knew that they would probably have to do his work for him, at great speed, to rattle out a bunch of clichés in his inimitable style, as the deadline loomed — it was the right thing to do and a sign of the comradeship which prevailed among the press corps at that time.

But he had already written something.

As they approached the slumped figure, they could see that he had indeed been able to type something on the sheet of paper which he had somehow wedged into the typewriter.

'Last night in the Ta' Qali Stadium' … it began.

And that's all he wrote.

Chapter 7 ~

| RED RED WINE

Joe Elliott of Def Leppard wasn't the only rock star who was spending time in Ireland in the 1980s. Charlie Haughey's tax exemption for artists had also benefited various members of Frankie Goes To Hollywood and Spandau Ballet and Mike Scott and the Waterboys and Sting and Elvis Costello and of course the other members of Def Leppard, who were somehow able to cope with life in a buggered economy in which condoms couldn't be displayed in a public place and where you couldn't get a divorce and which depended on Europe to do the heavy lifting in dark areas such as the legalisation of homosexuality.

The exemption also helped our own native rock stars to come to terms with the realities of living and working in Ireland. In fact, most of them seemed to be inordinately happy here, for various reasons which demonstrate that there is perhaps more to a country than just getting a good review from the IMF.

I had 'discovered' Frankie Goes To Hollywood when they were on the cusp of their phenomenal success with their first single, 'Relax' — though in truth, I was not the first to discover them and had never actually heard of them until I was sent by *Hot Press* to interview them in Liverpool. They were extraordinarily kind to me anyway, spending the day showing me around the city, introducing me to various Liverpool exotics and showing me the new video of the single which would soon be number one in every country in the world in which people have money. And which would make them enough money of their own to bring them to Ireland so that they could pay no tax on it.

They were among the nicest rock stars I have met, especially when you consider that they weren't actually stars yet, so they had nothing to protect. In fact, singer Holly insisted on seeing me off at Speke Airport as if I were a personal guest of theirs, remarking wistfully: 'I love airports, lad. You always feel you're going somewhere ...' A few weeks later, he was on a one-way ticket to the stratosphere, baby!

But the idea that there was a better world elsewhere would only partly explain their eventual affinity with Ireland and the Irish. Being from Liverpool, they were already Irish in ways that they probably didn't even realise. So deeply have the Irish embedded themselves in that great football city, you can walk round Liverpool today and see 'Irish' things and encounter 'Irish' people that you would hardly see in Ireland any more. A lot of this would be in the area of drinking and socialising in general, in a deep but strangely attractive melancholia and an alienation from England in general — and they've had a few decent bands, too.

So the Frankies, when they came to the actual island of Ireland, were just coming home — probably to a place that was becoming more fashionable than their own.

In fact, years later I did another interview with the three hetero-sexual members of the group, who spoke movingly of how they had found themselves for a while living in Co. Kilkenny, where the owner of the local video store had assured them he could get them any amount of hard-core pornography that they needed — 'the serious fucking donkey stuff'.

Sheffield, too, was a great old football city, but Joe Elliott was discovering the spirit of gracious living which pervaded Killiney Hill, with Bono up the road and maybe Adam Clayton dropping around on his way back to his stately home in Rathfarnham for a rap and a night-cap. And Van the Man was holed up there somewhere.

Joe would also find a girlfriend here, Karla. So despite the various amendments to the Constitution which were causing such a distraction, and despite innumerable letters to the *Irish Times* arguing about the exact point at which human life begins, about foetuses and zygotes and the morning-after pill, Ireland was now producing women who were acceptable to long-haired men wearing leather trousers, who had made millions out of heavy metal, and who were preparing to stride through the arenas of the United States along with their buddies, singing 'Pour Some Sugar On Me'.

Yes, we have established that sometimes, Paddy can't make it on his own. But here we are also establishing that there are a lot of folks out there who can't make it without Paddy. For a Joe Elliott, a season ticket to Bramall Lane and a grand house which used to belong to some Sheffield steel magnate might have its attractions, but there is also a lot to be said for quaffing at the top table in the Pink Elephant after a session in the Dockers, that pub beside the Windmill Lane studios where I had kindly agreed to write Paul McGrath's autobiography.

And the excellence of the Windmill Lane Studios meant that these men, if they really felt the need, could lay down some tracks in a fully professional environment, before resuming the onerous task of enjoying all the money they weren't giving to the taxman, thanks to C.J. Haughey and his love of the arts.

————

UB40 needed no encouragement at all to come and to make sweet reggae music at the studio in which U2 had made mega-platinum albums, but it would become increasingly difficult for them to strike the work-life balance. Singer Ali Campbell would later quit drinking that red, red wine. He would also speak wisely about his alcoholism, which had no doubt substantially 'progressed' during those happy times in the 1980s in Dublin town.

And the visiting stars were always ably assisted in their endeavours by the local variety, of which there were now many. Every week it seemed that a few local boys had been signed up by a major label, whose A&R men were swarming through the pubs of Dublin looking for the next U2, talking a lot of shit and consuming fantastic quantities of drink and drugs. George Byrne, whose inexhaustible passion for guitar-based American pop is matched only by a wintry eye for rock's follies, would learn of bands who had slipped a copy of their demo to some visiting record company potentate, along with a small gift of cocaine to help him make it through the night, but which would only ensure that he left the demo behind him in some Leeson Street toilet and that all information pertaining to the band would have entirely vanished from his mind by the time he got back to London, tired but happy.

For the artistes who made it through these trials, there might be a few weeks in which they would be worth a theoretical half-a-million quid. A magical time in which they would be high on the improbability of it all, until such time as the A&R man sobered up and thought better of his lost weekend in Dublin, or until they fired his ass and some other geezer set about the gloomy task of reversing all the decisions he had made.

Still, for a few moments back then, men could dream. They could dream of sitting in the Bailey or the Rajdoot Tandoori rapping with the Frankies, or hanging out in the Pink with Gary Kemp. Or maybe Sting. Drinking Harvey Wallbangers in the middle of the night with half of UB40 and thinking that it must be their turn next.

Suddenly there were things in Ireland that had never been seen before, such as folks arriving over here to view the graffiti on the wall of Windmill Lane and to add their own insignia. And there were things being done that were never done before, such as 'house-sitting'. Around this time I heard that someone had a job which entailed living in the house of a rock star in South Dublin while the rock star was away on tour.

Ireland had acquired its first house-sitters.

It was a way of life we had associated only with the ridiculously rich of American showbusiness, yet there were now Irishmen and women who were gainfully employed living in other people's mansions, most of them in the general direction of Killiney Hill. There were men living like rock stars who were not themselves rock stars, doing all the good stuff that rock stars do in their jacuzzis and their vast four-poster beds with the mirrored ceilings and their Maseratis, and doing none of the bad stuff, like trying to write songs for the new album when they'd prefer to be out enjoying themselves, or disgracing themselves at the MTV awards.

I mention these things to question again the accepted narrative of the 1980s in Ireland, that this was a time of almost uninterrupted bleakness, a line that has been asserted so often that it just can't be completely true. I have even been known to assert it myself.

Yet if we get beyond the received wisdom, we can see that the bleakness wasn't uninterrupted. In fact it was interrupted quite a lot, which would perhaps make the bleakness seem all the more stark when it resumed. But which should be remembered regardless.

We were moving from the darkness to the light, and back to the darkness all the time. And while the light was coming from some strange places, it was football, the old Republic, which had brought us a night as dark as it gets without anyone dying.

I refer to that night in Brussels in 1981, Belgium v the Republic, which seemed to set the tone for much of the decade to come, an occasion of unparalleled ugliness, not just for the brutal nature of the defeat, but in the light of what was subsequently learned by Paul Howard, then a journalist with the *Sunday Tribune*. In 2002, in his piece 'I Wanted Ireland to Win this Game', Howard felt compelled to revisit those terrible visions of thunder and lightning and incessant rain when the referee gave the Belgians a dodgy free-kick with three minutes to go, which they scored, to keep perhaps the best Irish eleven we ever had out of the 1982 World Cup.

And while that image of Eoin Hand with his head in his hands has defined that night, we tend to forget the earlier and more appalling injustice when a clearly legitimate Frank Stapleton goal was disallowed for offside by the Portuguese referee, one Raul Nazare.

For the purposes of his *Tribune* piece, Paul Howard tracked Nazare down to his home in Lisbon, where he was living comfortably in retirement — or at least he had been, until the Howmeister came to call with a video-tape of the match in question and a burning need to ask this Raul Nazare how in the name of God he could have done this to us?

It would break your heart.

In fact, Nazare remembers the Republic striker Mickey Walsh, whom he knew from Portuguese football, going to him after the match and saying, 'the hearts of the Irish people are crying'. Actually, Walsh called him a cheat. Then Liam Brady asked Walsh what the Portuguese word for thief was and confronted him with that.

Eoin Hand, who gave his personal copy of the video to Howard, recalls saying to Nazare: 'You're a disgrace. You've been paid off. You've robbed us.'

So, 21 years later, Nazare accepted Howard's invitation to look again at the video, to watch it on the television in his own apartment and to explain what he did to us that night.

At first Nazare is adamant that Stapleton was offside and that it was the linesman who made the decision. Then something else occurs to him. 'I remember now that I had blown the whistle before Stapleton touched the ball. So technically, you see, I did not disallow the goal, there was no goal to disallow.'

The two men look at the tape again, now joined by Nazare's daughter Elsa and her husband, Antonio. Ireland have a free-kick on the edge of the penalty box. Brady is standing over the ball, Stapleton loitering around the penalty spot. Just before Brady chips the ball into the box, Stapleton makes a run for the near post, beats the goalkeeper to the ball and side-foots it into the net. He is a mile onside. The whistle is blown after the goal is scored.

Nazare, as though disbelieving what he is seeing, asks to see it again.

He looks at it a third time, his eyes now six inches from the screen.

Clearly the linesman does not signal at all until a good three seconds after Nazare himself disallowed the goal, at which point he guiltily raises the flag.

'I think I made a mistake when I told you it was offside', Nazare concedes, but now he claims he had given an indirect free-kick and that the goal was disallowed because Brady scored direct.

Except it is clear that the ball changes direction on its way into the net, due to Stapleton hitting it.

Awkwardly for Nazare, his own daughter tells him that he couldn't be right about that — though her husband Antonio is sticking with the old man, Antonio being in the business of selling slow-motion technology to TV companies and thus an expert on this sort of thing.

Eventually they find a smaller TV in another room, but now it is even clearer that Brady did not score direct.

Then Nazare remembers something else. He reacts as if he can't believe he had forgotten this — 'the ball hits off me,' he declares. 'It hits off my back and goes into the goal.'

So now he's saying that the ball changes direction because it hits him, not Stapleton. In fact, when the kick is taken, he is running backwards towards the six-yard box and collides with the centre-half Walter Meeuws.

Howard believes it is doubtful that Nazare even saw the goal, and his most charitable suggestion is that he may have instinctively disallowed it because he had hampered Walter Meeuws.

By now the four of them, in the apartment in Lisbon, are choreographing the scene and Nazare is still working on his defence: 'I'm in the penalty box, where I shouldn't be,' he says. 'Frank pushes me and he turns me. And when I turn, the ball hits off my back and it goes into the goal. I remember now.'

Ah, it would break your heart.

Perhaps it was this crushing sense of disappointment, of our old friend failure, that ultimately bred the success which Paul Howard now enjoys as Ross O'Carroll-Kelly, one of the most celebrated creations in the history of Irish publishing.

Nonetheless, if perchance your heart wasn't totally broken by that meeting with Raul Nazare, I am told by my friend Dion Fanning, now a leading sportswriter, that he was nine years old when that match was played and that he has a clear recollection of angrily tearing a picture of the by-now-infamous Nazare out of a Sunday paper and ripping it to pieces. He planned to assemble the pieces into an effigy, and burn it. But he couldn't find a box of matches.

The kid had made his point. But the result stood, and we would not be going to Spain in '82.

It is tempting to see that episode as the defining narrative of Ireland's misfortune throughout the 1980s, when it seemed that we had been excluded from life's feast. Perhaps we are also drawn to it because it has a terrible injustice at its core, giving us the feeling that it wasn't our fault, that we were done down by the badness of others. Which we know was not the truth in the case of all things that went wrong for us at that time, but which somehow consoles us.

And astonishingly, nearly thirty years later, we were still getting done out of the World Cup. Indeed Frank Stapleton, scorer of goals-that-were-disallowed-for-no-reason-at-all, would testify that the

2009 Thierry Henry episode was not even the first time we had been done out of it in Paris. You could say it was actually the third time in Paris alone, if you counted a 1-0 defeat to Spain in a play-off for the 1966 World Cup which was held in Paris because the FAI apparently took the Spanish shilling and gave them what was effectively 'home' advantage.

But let us be rigorously honest: when France cheated us out of that place in the 2010 World Cup, many of us were privately fearing that they would have second thoughts and agree to play us again, in which case they would most certainly beat us out the door and take away our only consolation, the ecstasy of victimhood.

——

So this is an endlessly recurring theme, one that isn't exclusive to the 1980s. And there was further consolation back then, because it wasn't all bad anyway. I went to the Bruce Springsteen concert in Slane in the back of a van with a *Hot Press* crew that included lay-out man Leo Regan, who would later compile a stunningly courageous book of photo-journalism about white nazis in England and make award-winning TV documentaries, but whose main cultural contribution on the day was to introduce me to the music of The Pogues.

Yes, it was in the back of a van on the way to Slane, on a dazzlingly sunny Saturday morning in the summer of 1985, with about three beers already on board, that I first heard 'Streams of Whiskey'. It was a piercingly beautiful moment and almost everyone who went to see Springsteen that day remembers such moments of their own.

But not entirely unpredictably, many of those memories are polluted by something that Springsteen himself noted, something of which he spoke privately: the amazing amount of drinking he witnessed among the Irish.

Ah, even on that long, long day of almost supernatural lightness, the darkness was never too far away from us.

———

Dermot Morgan, more than any other figure of that time, seems to me to personify this constant drifting between the darkness and the light and the darkness again.

Dermot always seemed to be living in the moment, and living well. He always behaved in a way a successful entertainer was supposed to behave. You would not see Dermot driving an old banger or keeping his hand in his pocket in the pub just because he had no income, as such. It was impossible to be in his company, and not to be greatly entertained.

Yet I got to know him at a time when there wasn't much going on in his career apart from recriminations with RTÉ over an infamous TV special which was supposed to have been a full series, but which had been chopped down to a one-hour special for reasons which Dermot found outrageous: essentially RTÉ types were saying that they knew what was funny better than he. We have no way of knowing how wrong they were, or if indeed they were wrong at all.

Dermot loved football so much, in the League of Ireland he supported UCD — 'I don't like crowds', he would explain. And we might even suspect that his affinity with the garrison game had gone against him or at least made it easier to dismiss him — his portrayal of a mad hurler jumping out of the studio audience to remonstrate with Pat Kenny would have made traditionalists feel uneasy. But it was certainly worth talking about, on the record, to the injured party. Apart from this dark episode with RTÉ, there was a sense that Morgan's predicament said a lot about the country in general, how Ireland had a way of dumping on anyone who was any good.

I would look at the likes of Paul Hogan, the Australian comic who was then becoming an international star, who was clearly not as talented as Dermot but who had got himself to a place where the talent he had could be released. Why the hell couldn't Dermot Morgan do that, too, instead of wasting his time and his energy arguing with RTÉ, with bloody civil servants?

Dermot picked me up outside Blackrock DART station in whatever fine motor he was driving at that time and drove up the hills to the Blue Light pub in Barnacullia, which would later become internationally known as the place in which Adam Clayton was busted in the car-park for possession of dope — Adam would later acknowledge his addiction to alcohol and other substances, but at the time, like so many of us, he was just working on it.

Dermot, who oddly enough was free of all the usual addictions, drove up there entirely in the character of Eamon Dunphy. He was a deeply, deeply funny Dunphy, and given his obsession with football, he was particularly exercised at the time with an interview I had done in which Dunphy had monstered some of his sports-writing colleagues, calling them 'scabrous wretches'. He would later characterise them as 'the fans with typewriters', but 'scabrous wretches' was better, and Morgan loved it. 'Scabrous wretch! Scabrous wretch!' he would holler at every possible opportunity.

Yet while he was riffing anarchically, Dermot would also ask you not to smoke in the car. Probably for health reasons, possibly because he was ahead of his time — back then in Ireland even if the driver was on the point of death due to emphysema, he would be reluctant to ask you not to smoke. He wouldn't want to upset you. He would prefer to die than to interfere with your enjoyment.

Dermot didn't subscribe to that particular sort of moral cowardice. And he was also quite proper in other ways, which are usually described as middle-class. For example, he was one of the few men in the history of Ireland to send thank-you notes. Then again he might ring you up and frighten you by pretending to be some dreaded individual such as a bank manager, intoning something about your expenditure getting out of control and concerns at head office — you got the impression he had been on the receiving end of a few such calls himself, so convincing was the style.

Like Dunphy, he was full of contradictions, but the contradiction that most concerns us here is that Dermot was a public performer who, in his youth, had allegedly suffered from agoraphobia. Usually agoraphobia is described as a fear of open spaces (again one thinks of the terraces at UCD) but as Dermot described it in the Blue Light that day, it was essentially a fear of leaving the house.

But when I raised the topic, Dermot asked me to pause the tape-recorder and to talk about it off the record. He was afraid of how it might look and maybe he was afraid that it would vindicate those in RTÉ whom he felt had damaged him — they could claim that the man was now admitting that maybe he had a few screws loose, that he was 'difficult'.

Maybe it was just a general fear of people knowing things about him that were really none of their business. Whatever the source of the fear, it was strong enough to keep the old agoraphobia off the record, for the time being at least — when he felt the time was right to talk about it, I would be the first to know. Maybe when he was a massive star, and they couldn't get him any more. Or maybe when Ireland was free.

It is truly extraordinary that in Ireland at that time a bright and sophisticated man would be afraid of such things, especially when you consider that we now live in a time in which men would be boasting loudly of such an ailment. Indeed they would be prepared to invent a spot of teenage agoraphobia to demonstrate how far they have travelled and the terrible obstacles that were in their way, how they had once been afraid to leave the house and now they were standing in front of 3,000 strangers telling funny stories.

They might build an entire career on the back of it.

But Dermot, who had the moral courage to ask passengers not to smoke in his car, was still spooked about the prevailing attitudes towards issues of mental illness. You could sense that deep fear in him, of the creepy forces that could destroy his fragile existence on a whim, that army of the Irish night, and the more mundane tormentors he would describe as 'the suits', permanent and pensionable.

That dead hand had touched so many in this country. It could even reach out and touch those who had escaped and made it to the other side, like John Giles. Back in the 1970s, when Giles was the most influential player in the most successful club side of the time, Leeds Utd, he would be routinely traduced as a man who regarded playing for his country not as a signal honour, but as a tiresome duty. And on the rare occasions when he deigned to play for us, his heart allegedly wasn't in it.

This was terrible bullshit, but it seemed to come naturally to the suits of football — the blazers to be exact — who found it reasonable for the players to arrive over from England on the boat the night before an important international match, having played a full match for their club the previous day, and to be grateful for the opportunity. Representing his country, supposedly the highest honour known to football man, a player would encounter conditions in which no serious professional should have been expected to work, and having created that morass, when the results were somehow poor, the suits and blazers would do what suits and blazers and other such respectably dressed men have always done — they would blame the talent.

Mercifully they were powerless to do serious damage to Giles, who had already made it. But if you were Dermot Morgan, in the late 1980s, the dead hand could destroy you, and he knew it.

Ah, if only he could have a bit of what they had, if only he had —

a job. It was said by Anthony Cronin of Patrick Kavanagh and it can be said of Dermot Morgan, too, that all he really needed was a job.

Perhaps he was too scatter-brained to work with in the 1980s, too undisciplined for the fantastic levels of precision needed in TV comedy. Perhaps he was 'difficult' or perhaps his hammering of the Provos made him a tricky proposition for the light-entertainment department. But even if they had given him all the professional help they could, in the most empathetic creative environment, they didn't give him the one thing that would have liberated him from so much grief — they didn't give him any sense of security. By this I don't mean the six-figure salary for life and the pension that they themselves would be on — I mean, let's not be silly here — I just mean some assurance that he could pay his bills for the vaguely foreseeable future, that he would be employed to produce comedy until such time as he got it right. By which time he wouldn't need them any more. Along with Gerard Stembridge, Pauline McLynn and Eoin Roe he would present them with a radio hit, *Scrap Saturday*, but in the end they didn't really want that either.

Dermot was not to know, in the depths of his own struggles, that the emigration of a generation would yield a massive result for him: it was Graham Linehan leaving for London and persuading Arthur Mathews to join him from which all else followed. I wish I could have told him that day in the Blue Light that I had these friends, who would one day write him an international hit, that it would all turn out great.

But Arthur and Graham themselves were still in the dark about that one.

———

A character called Father Ted Crilly was starting to form in Arthur's head and was being developed by himself and Graham and Paul Woodfull, the other lay-out man in the *Hot Press* at that time, in the context of a group called the Joshua Trio. It was being formed late at night during production weekends at the magazine, these insane work-marathons which as late as the late 1980s, would go something like this: you would get a few galleys containing an article and you would proof-read them, using a blue marker to highlight any wrong spellings. You would write these corrections on a sheet of paper and then you would walk down three flights of stairs to the typesetter, usually Jack Broder, a lady with a superb Mullingar accent, a type-setting wizard who was greatly in demand for her speed and her vast capacity for toil. Which may explain why she was starting to get other work, including a job typing up a first novel called *The South* by a journalist called Colm Tóibín.

Having given the corrections to Jack, you would walk back up the stairs to do some more proof-reading, maybe a few headlines and captions, before walking down the stairs again to collect the corrections, and walking back up the stairs to commence the task of cutting them out individually with a scalpel, applying cow-gum to the back of the sliver of paper and sticking the correction down on the page which Arthur or Paul had laid out. And you would do this, every second weekend, for most of the day and most of the night, the sessions broken up when a certain number of pages had been finished, enough for our leader Niall Stokes to lash together a package and run like the wind to his car in the hope of catching a van bound for the printers in Kerry.

Sometimes one of us would go with him, to keep him awake if the chase started stretching beyond Dublin, perhaps on into Munster. Hence the story of how Liam Mackey ended up running through Newbridge at three in the morning with his shoes in a biscuit tin.

It was all terribly simple really.

In hot pursuit of the van, Niall's car had run out of petrol in Newbridge and Liam had this idea of going to the garda station to ask for a container into which he might put petrol when he got to

Enjoying the view in Genoa. (*Inpho*)

Kevin Sheedy pulls the trigger. (*Inpho*)

Jack Charlton, Jack Charlton, Arnold O'Byrne of Opel and an uileann piper. It all made sense at the time. (*Image courtesy of Comhaltas Ceoltóiri Éireann* comhaltas.ie)

Father Ted, fondly remembered. (*Pictorial Press*)

The Singing Priest, Father Michael Cleary, not so fondly remembered. (*The Irish Times*)

A typical scene in Dublin city centre on match days during the Charlton years. (*RTÉ*)

Romania didn't have quite the same level of support. (*Inpho*)

Paul McGrath in the Stadio Olimpico. (*Inpho*)

Donal McCann and John Kavanagh in the Gate Theatre's production of *Juno and the Paycock* which reached Broadway during Euro 88. (*Corbis*)

u2, circa 1990. 'Put 'Em Under Pressure', produced by Larry, is probably the best football record ever made. (*Getty*)

John Aldridge scores
against Malta in
Valletta, and we are
through to Italia 90.
(*Sportsfile*)

The 1980s weren't all bad —
Springsteen at Slane, 1985.
(*Corbis*)

Bob Geldof and Bob Geldof. (*Getty*)

Jack (with megaphone) had Health and Safety concerns during the Homecoming. (*Inpho*)

Stephen Roche brought it all back home in 1987. (*Inpho*)

Jack Charlton, international celebrity. (*Inpho*)

RTÉ was rightly proud of its Italia 90 studio. (*RTÉ*)

Another great day for Ireland: Charles J. Haughey and Monsignor James Horan at Knock Airport. (*Courtesy of Ireland West Airport*)

The Pogues in 1987, the year of 'Fairytale of New York'. (*Corbis*)

The lads outside the Sant'Elia stadium, Cagliari. (*Inpho*)

Charles J. Haughey opens the International Financial Services Centre, which would boast a 'sophisticated and responsive regulatory environment'. (*The Irish Times*)

The dreaded Gullit. (*Inpho*)

My Left Foot, released in 1989, was nominated for five Oscars and won two. (*Alamy*)

Cardinal Cahal Daly meets the new boss. (*The Irish Times*)

Pavarotti's 'Nessun Dorma' ('None Shall Sleep') was the perfect soundtrack. (*Corbis*)

the petrol station further up the road. The gardaí gave him a biscuit tin.

As he ran towards the petrol station he found that his nice new white slip-on shoes kept slipping off, slowing him down when speed was of the essence. So he had the bright idea of taking off his nice shoes and putting them into the biscuit tin as he ran to the petrol station.

And that is why Liam Mackey was running through Newbridge at three in the morning with his shoes in a biscuit tin.

———

It is also worth reflecting on the fact that we were regularly passing comment on the somewhat backward approach of Jack Charlton's Ireland, while we ourselves were still living in an Ireland in which we stuck our corrections down with glue. We were questioning Jack's strange attachment to the primitive methods of Mick McCarthy at centre-half, while at the cutting edge of the new media we were interviewing people using tape recorders which were as big and heavy as the average refrigerator and which didn't work half the time because the batteries were dead.

And at all times, like everyone else who had the best interests of Irish football at heart, we feared for the health and well-being of Paul McGrath, as we sat downstairs in the International smoking incessantly and drinking pints, night after night.

In this working environment, it seemed unthinkable that a fully-formed magazine could appear once a fortnight, every fortnight of the year. Yet the *Hot Press* not only survived, it is still there after more than 30 years, and unlike *In Dublin* or *Magill* it has continued uninterrupted for all that time. Even when the country was being destroyed again in the 1980s, on the football field and in every other field, you had at least three high-class publications describing how it was being done and who was doing it and what should be done to them.

Again I say that success breeds success, but failure also has its part to play.

Hot Press was in at the start of the biggest Irish story of the time, on about forty different levels — the U2 story — while *Magill* was covering the old, dead culture peopled by Fianna Fáil and Fine Gael. And in their spare time, *Hot Press* even did the best political piece of the decade, John Waters' interview with Charles Haughey. It was also the only publication that Paul McGrath would talk to for a long time. So it was ahead of the game in seeing this synergy between 'pop culture' as it is disparagingly known and football, recognising the fact that many of us were as devoted to our club and country as we were to our record collections. And that these things mattered more than most things in this life.

It was as natural for George Byrne, Arthur Mathews, Damian Corless, Ian O'Doherty, Liam Mackey, Niall Stokes or myself to be talking about Jack's deployment of Maurice Setters as it was for journalists closer to Leinster House to be talking about the composition of the shadow cabinet. We spoke routinely of fabled FAI characters such as 'Big Dinners' and 'Little Dinners', and we knew exactly what Ray Treacy meant when he said, 'I got forty-three caps for Ireland, probably about forty of them against Poland' — apparently the FAI had lucked in to a superior brand of hospitality offered by the Poles and so we kept playing them, especially away, often to no apparent purpose.

'Myself and Tomascevski were like blood brothers and most of the players knew each other by their first names', Treacy recalled in Paul Rowan's fine book, *The Team That Jack Built*. 'We'd kick in down the same end before the match.' As Rowan explained, Poland was a great place to buy cheap cut-glass, and one council member of that time used to buy ladies' underwear in bulk from Poland, for sale back in Ireland.

This stuff was just as important to us as the new Graham Parker album, and it all got into the magazine somehow, ensuring that it wasn't just an information sheet for musos, it had — to reduce it to the simplest analysis — a bit of everything.

Informed above all by rock 'n' roll music, in this *Hot Press* was broadly in touch with the Irish character, which has a remarkable affinity with both the music and the spirit of rock 'n' roll, to the extent that it is one of the few areas of life in which we can honestly claim to be world leaders. But the paper was also touched by genius from the beginning, and perhaps that is what made all the difference.

Bill Graham was the name of the genius in question, and there was no-one of Bill's calibre at *In Dublin* or *Magill* because there was no-one of Bill's calibre anywhere. He was a deeply original thinker and an inordinately civilised man who could make the most apparently ludicrous connections fit together — Spandau Ballet ... The RTÉ autumn schedule ... Headage payments!! You might get it, if you thought about it for twenty minutes, but Bill seemed to make these connections effortlessly, with a great knowing grin and a loud Northern exclamation: *ahahhh*! He would wait for your acknowledgment of how right he was, as if he had just made a childishly obvious remark about the weather.

Flann O'Brien has been described as 'myriad-minded' and that would describe Bill, too. His brain was wired differently to the rest of us, and to be dazzled by its splendour from an early age was a joy, a challenge and a privilege. That a man of Bill's intellectual prowess had devoted himself mainly to writing about 'youth culture', and the Irish variety in particular, should tell you all you need to know about what was important at that time, and what was not.

Even now, in the midst of some national trauma, people who knew Bill try to imagine what he would have made of it, what shard of original thinking he would produce — he remains a sort of posthumous Supreme Court, to whom we go for the final verdict.

He was convinced that most Irish musicians needed to have better record collections, that they just hadn't been exposed to enough of the right influences. And rather than simply pointing this out from his lofty critical perch, he would meet them in bars and give them his own albums, which had been played on his own primitive Dansette — Bill wasn't a man for admiring the way the sound of Pink Floyd filled the room with quadrophonic glory, he was listening for the raw essence.

A big man in a blue corduroy jacket with a wild look reminiscent of Jack Nicholson, he thought he was the greatest dancer, though the beat he was following seemed to exist only in his own head.

He was one of about three men in Ireland with a deep knowledge and a love of black music.

A large section of the music business simply thought him mad, but I would remind you that there were at least five of these people who would always listen very carefully to what Bill said — these would be the four members of U2 and their manager, who were brought together by Bill.

In fact, if there is one thing above all others which marks them out as superior beings, it is the sincere regard they had for Bill. And when he died suddenly on the morning of the Cup Final in 1996, they came over from Miami to pay their respects. And Gavin Friday sang 'Tower of Song' in the church in Howth, which was also a bit special.

'The night will not be the same,' Gavin said.

There is not a lot of great writing about the Tiger years, but there would have been if Bill had stuck around. And for those who were growing up in the 1980s, reading *Hot Press*, Bill provided this service: he improved your mind. And he also drank pints of Guinness a fair bit, on borrowed fivers, and was late with his copy when it all got too much for him, which could cause further complications at the lay-out desks and in the proof-reading department.

So in this working environment, deep into the night, there would be singing. It was extraordinarily like those scenes in movies in which men start singing a negro spiritual, except here the lonely cry of the human heart would come from Paul Woodfull or Arthur perhaps working on a lounge-music adaptation of a U2 song for the Joshua Trio. They were starting to do these numbers in public in the Baggot Inn, interspersed with various musings from this guy Father Ted Crilly, played by Arthur.

But it would be a long time yet, before the connection was made with the man who was still paying his own dues on that day in the Blue Light.

Dermot's big idea at the time — one of them, anyway — was actually a story of how Irish football had brought the best out of the people in a dark time. But it didn't happen in the 1980s, it was a story from the 1950s of how the omnipotent Archbishop of Dublin, John Charles McQuaid, had expressed his disapproval of the proposed visit to Dalymount Park of Yugoslavia, a team which, in the eyes of McQuaid, represented the forces of a communist regime which was persecuting Catholics and should therefore be spurned by all Irish people.

Generally at that time if McQuaid expressed disapproval of anything, it would be studiously avoided by all members of the ruling class and anyone else who knew what was good for them, but a crowd of 22,000 turned out that day, giving out a great roar of Dublin working-class defiance of the ogre McQuaid, or anyone else who would deny them the great joy of their lives that was association football. And turning a predictable 4-1 defeat into a great day for Ireland.

Dermot loved that story, but he couldn't drum up enough interest in making a movie out of it, or a TV drama or whatever. So he continued on, constantly trying to get something started, rounding up anyone in Dublin with any sense of humour at all, meeting in hotels and making big plans.

Though it would be whispered that he was 'unprofessional', in a larger sense he was perhaps the only true professional in a place full of amateurs.

Like the Republic he kept getting the bad breaks, but there was something different about Dermot, something that the football team probably doesn't have to this day — he would never be content with the moral victories. He really felt that there was a million bucks out there with his name on it, and that he was going to get there eventually. Unlike the Republic, the lads who would turn back so many times at the gates of the promised land, when the time came, he would be able to take that extra step. He wasn't afraid of it.

Chapter 8

A SOPHISTICATED AND RESPONSIVE REGULATORY ENVIRONMENT

They say that politics and football don't mix, but of course that is twaddle. In fact, if we know nothing else about this world, we know that politics and football mix, all the time.

Yet at the time of Jack's appointment, so sad was the state of Irish football and of Ireland in general, that politics and football genuinely weren't mixing. In fact, far from mixing with it, few politicians would care to recognise the existence of the game, because there was really nothing in it for them.

This hadn't always been the case. We have already alluded to the roaring 1950s' controversy over the visit by communist Yugoslavia — which may seem like a religious matter, though of course at the time religion *was* politics: religion was just about everything. But traditionally the Church favoured Gaelic games, with the Archbishop of Cashel and Emly throwing in the ball for the All-Ireland hurling final and the minor football final, and the Artane Boys Band entertaining the crowd at Croke Park with their march medleys, with no mention of the fact that Artane was one of the institutions run by the Church and the State in which poor children were routinely abused physically and sexually. At Dalymount Park we preferred the music of the free men of the St James Brass and Reed band.

Admittedly, there has been a suggestion of bad politics in the legend that the Republic was the first country to offer to play

Germany after the Second World War, which is allegedly the reason that the 'away' strip of the Germans is green — a sort of tribute to Paddy for reaching out to the fallen Fatherland. It is a lovely story but, as far as we can ascertain, it is not true. Switzerland was actually the first country to play Germany after World War 2. Though it has to be said that a reasonable percentage of people in Ireland at that time would have been proud to have the Germans wearing the green, both home and away.

In the 'modern' era, until Jack started getting a few big results, for a long time, one of the few Irish politicians who would openly be associated with the Republic's football team was David Andrews. As you waited for the kick-off in Dalymount, reading the official match programme, you would see Andrews' name as Patron of the FAI. It would look quite impressive — Andrews, after all, was the scion of a leading Fianna Fáil family, a distinguished-looking cove.

But if you looked a little bit closer, you would realise that Andrews' association with the FAI did not necessarily mean much in the greater Fianna Fáil scheme of things. He was, after all, marginalised on the 'liberal' wing of the party, opposed to the leadership of Charles Haughey for all sorts of reasons, not all of them good, and to complete the stereotype, he represented the borough of Dun Laoghaire, which, in the eyes of many of his colleagues, would make him a West Brit and thus the right man to be endorsing the garrison game.

For a long time, Official Ireland, as it was christened by Eamon Dunphy, had stayed away from the garrison game, but with Italia 90 coming down the track, that time was about to end.

———

It would be wrong to think that Haughey preferred Gaelic games to football, as such. He had played Gaelic football in his youth and he would feel it was in his interest to be seen in Croke Park rather than in Lansdowne Road, but I don't think Haughey had much interest in sport anyway. At least, not in the ball-games of the masses. He had refused invitations to Lansdowne Road, fearing it might upset his followers, with all its associations with 'foreign games'. In his mature years he favoured the pastimes of the gentry, the hunting and the shooting and the sailing, partly due to his exalted image of himself and the lifestyle he felt appropriate for a man of his stature, and partly for more deep-rooted psychological reasons. You could never imagine Haughey playing golf, for example. It is too humbling. It exposes human weakness too horribly and its image is too middle class — Haughey didn't see himself as middle class, but as an aristocrat. So instead of thrashing around in a bunker and wheeling his trolley around the links with other men who might well include a taxi-driver, Haughey preferred to equip himself for his sporting endeavours with a horse, or a boat, or a gun.

He had materialised on the podium to hail Stephen Roche's win in the Tour de France, but there was a hint of cosmopolitan glamour to this — it was Paris, after all — and he had done this for the usual venal motives which compel politicians to associate themselves with sporting success, or just to have their picture taken, yet there was something almost inspiring about the lengths to which he was prepared to go in this case. Only a country that is completely desperate for something good to happen to it, could imagine their Prime Minister travelling to another country in this way, to seize his moment.

We really needed it, and he was able to recognise that need.

We had lived in a world of bullshit for so long, that when something of this magnitude happened, and it *wasn't* bullshit, it was almost too much for us, and for our leader, to take in. Especially when the leader in question had been instrumental in perpetuating so much of that bullshit.

He was a man of almost unlimited appetites in relation to food, drink and sex, yet his governments would hold the line against the 'liberal agenda' which he himself had been following to the full extent of his capabilities for most of his adult life, along with a few agendas of his own which the most far-seeing liberals wouldn't even have contemplated.

Not that a leader should necessarily be a virtuous man, or a consistent man, but the gap between the public and the private Haughey was remarkable. And yet he kept us darkly entertained with the grandeur of the deception — the sophisticated statesman who was paralysed with fear of doing anything that might upset the most backward of his followers; the lord in his mansion telling us we were living above our means. And this was before we were fully aware that Haughey was 'rich' only to the extent that he could get people who were actually rich to bung him bucketfuls of money.

Yes, it was probably the size of the lies that entertained so many of us, that made us recognise in Haughey some essential characteristic of our tribe, some inexhaustible and ineradicable strain of bullshit.

———

My one encounter with The Boss was actually quite pleasant. It was back in 1986, not long after the arrival of Jack, and the actual purpose of my visit to Leinster House was to interview the Foreign Minister of Nicaragua, Father Miguel d'Escoto. He was over here with a delegation from the Sandinista government, the Sandinistas being so hot at the time, The Clash had named an album after them. It was not unknown for young Irish people to go over there to join in the spirit of the revolution which had deposed the evil old American-backed Somoza regime. Which probably wasn't as leisurely as a summer spent in Puerto Banus, but perhaps a tad more character-forming. The writer Joseph O'Connor went there, and it became the setting for his novel *Desperadoes*.

O'Connor would eventually write powerful stuff about the Irish at the World Cup in America, but in 1986, that was an unimaginable journey.

Our new football supremo, Jack, would not have realised it, but he was coming to a country in which people were so desperate to find something to support that was even half-decent, the best of them would take themselves off to the badlands of Central America to seek it.

In fact, few of us realised the true potential of a successful Ireland football team because Haughey's Ireland, and indeed Garret FitzGerald's Ireland, had dissipated our energies in so many other ways, we could no longer imagine the nation coming together for any purpose. In our hearts there was a hole the size of Nicaragua, and as far as we could tell, Jack Charlton wouldn't be doing much to fill it.

We were wrong about that. But it seemed pretty unpromising at the time, with most of our good players getting older and Jack only getting the job after a deeply twisted voting procedure, an FAI cock-up in the grand style which was best described by Liam 'Rashers' Tuohy, one of the unsuccessful candidates. 'It was a two-horse race', he said. 'And I finished fourth.'

There was no sane reason in 1986 to hope that a soaring new vision of our country might emerge from the general direction of Merrion Square, or indeed from Leinster House, which was just a few yards away from the powerhouse of Irish football, so some of us would be looking instead to the Sandinistas for a vision of a risen people. They had defied the United States of America, a superpower which lived just up the road from them, while we were arguing about the Kerry Babies. They had replaced the disgraceful Somoza with the impressive Ortega, while we were thinking of replacing the illustrious Liam Brady with some busy little geezer from Oxford Utd called Houghton.

And their Foreign Minister was a priest, but no Father Michael Cleary he.

The interview had been arranged with *Hot Press* by Michael D. Higgins, and I was told it would be done 'over lunch'. So I was expecting a few minutes with the distinguished cleric while we ate egg and chips in the cafeteria and railed against the evils of the Reagan administration, only to discover on my arrival at Leinster House that contrary to all my expectations this would be quite an elegant affair, a full dinner for about ten people with several courses and waiters pouring drops of wine into your glass for you to taste and to offer your approval, before they filled it.

Introduced to the Foreign Minister by Michael D., I did the interview at the side of the room while they were having the aperitifs. He talked up a storm, did Father D'Escoto, about Reagan's dirty war, while I sipped a Campari.

Then I found myself sitting down to the first course with the distinguished visitors and our own representatives, including Gerard Collins of Fianna Fáil, then out of government, leaving Gerard free to be eating big dinners with the revolutionary intellectuals of Central America. I seem to recall some humorous discussion taking place about Irish sausages and their significance in our culture, with Collins asking the waiter if some sausages could be produced for our guests — 'pig-meat' he added for the benefit of the Nicaraguans — perhaps momentarily forgetting that Father D'Escoto was a highly-educated Catholic priest who had probably figured out somewhere along the line that sausages are made of pig-meat. But at least Collins was there: to his eternal discredit, Garret FitzGerald who was then Taoiseach, was a no-show.

Haughey came in, about halfway through, for all the world as if he was still the man in charge, which in his mind he probably was.

First, he had some bad news. 'There has been an explosion at a nuclear reactor in the Soviet Union,' he intoned, standing at the top of the table.

Thus I heard the news about Chernobyl, from Charles Haughey. It was not looking good. Then he turned to Michael D.: 'You were right about that nuclear thing all the time, Michael D.,' he said, and then he quipped good-naturedly: 'Now why don't you do the right thing and leave that bloody party . . ?'

Haughey had apparently always felt that a man of Michael D.'s calibre was wasted in the Labour Party, and perhaps he longed to have him on his side if only as a companion, someone he could regard as an equal. A man unlike the gobshites in his own party, a man to whom he could talk about the finer things in life.

Which might or might not include Michael D.'s long association with Galway Utd football club. It is not widely known that Michael D. has any association with Galway Utd though he is actually the President of the grand old club. And the fact that it is not widely known says much about the man himself and the restraint he would show in the years to come, when colleagues who knew nothing and cared less about football would be disporting themselves in executive boxes, claiming ownership of the Boys In Green in the company of Corporate Paddy. Their good buddy.

Michael D. would be not be along for that ride.

As he introduced me to Haughey and we shook hands, I thought I felt a weakness come over him at the mention of the words *Hot Press*, perhaps a flashback to his infamous John Waters interview in which Haughey had said 'fuck' a lot, and which had done him no harm — though the memory of all those unguarded remarks appearing across several pages of the magazine may have haunted him still. In truth, it was actually quite a statesmanlike little appearance, especially given the gracelessness of the Fine Gael absence — maybe Garret was out there formulating the Fine Gael response to Chernobyl.

Haughey was back in the saddle in 1987, with Fine Gael, now under Alan Dukes, having formulated the Tallaght Strategy, a fancy name given to the policy of allowing Haughey to run the country without Fine Gael indulging in asinine opposition just for the sake of it, as long as Haughey did the right things. The responsible things.

Then in 1989, after a bad election call, Haughey found himself, incredibly, in coalition with Des O'Malley, the man to whom he was thought to be referring in that *Hot Press* interview when he said that there were some fuckers whose throats he'd like to cut, fuckers he would like to throw over the edge of a fucking cliff.

Now this fucker was his partner in government.

According to Official Ireland, everything started to change around this time. According to received wisdom, in the late 1980s Haughey, with the greatest reluctance, finally put aside all the bullshit and started to face the truth about the state of economy, to accept that it was completely and utterly fucked and actually to do something about it.

And according to Official Ireland, this, allied to the improved sense of national well-being which was being created by various Irish successes, most notably those of U2 and the football team under the Gruff Yorkshireman, would set the country on the right road.

And that road would eventually lead to this thing called the Celtic Tiger.

———

Neat.

Maybe too neat.

Maybe, in fact, more bullshit.

Here's an alternative reading of the situation, by Gene Kerrigan, in a *Sunday Independent* column in 2009 in which he reflects on the calibre of Ireland's elite and their version of history:

The first generation of leaders having achieved independence, weren't sure what to do with it. Thus, the country stagnated for several decades, dependent on emigration for survival.

In those days the elite included the Catholic Church. The priority for the bishops was to safeguard their power — to the point of protecting the abusers of children. In business it was the era of cute hoors, building small local dynasties. In politics, it was a time of placeholders.

Then came Haughey — a bright man, who hadn't a new idea since the 1960s. He was a taker, and he took incessantly, lost in self-aggrandisement.

To today's media cheerleaders, the late 1980s was the time when political leaders took 'tough decisions' and restored balance to public finances. To some of us, that era looks somewhat different. It was a period of massive, complex criminal tax frauds, organised by bankers and engaged in by thousands of 'respectable' people from the comfortable classes, at a cost to the State of hundreds of millions of pounds. The roll-call of criminality is studded with household names, in politics and business.

At the time, many within the elite — in the professions, in politics, even in the Central Bank — knew about the frauds.

There was no 'tough decision' to confront this criminal assault on the republic. Instead the health and education of the punters, the skulls, the eejits, bore the brunt. In a traumatised health service, people died prematurely, unnecessarily, cruelly.

Our leaders stood not with us, but with the criminals. In some cases they were the criminals.

The police, as always when the elite are involved, found something else to do. (Jailing street traders was a biggie.)

If allegations can't be ignored, tribunals are set up — to last years, costing millions, too often leading absolutely nowhere.

The professions service and benefit from this state of affairs. The academics too. The media picks a hero from the ranks of the powerful and cheerleads.

The past 20 years have been dominated ideologically by the PDS and Charlie McCreevy, who mimicked the idea of the then-fashionable Thatcher and Reagan 'revolution'. This involved wrecking the tax base and unwinding the regulatory reforms that followed the Great Depression and stabilised capitalism for 40 years.

It could be summarised as, 'let's free the imagination of the entrepreneur from the dead hand of bureaucratic regulation'.

Oh, I see.

And how did that turn out?

A slightly different narrative there, a subtle shift of emphasis.

Kerrigan was focusing on the political and economic trends of the time. Sport and culture were getting on with it, as best they could. And as we have seen, their best could be very good indeed — let us remind ourselves that in the opening pages we were looking at The Gate on Broadway and Christy Moore at the Carnegie Hall and *My Left Foot* and 'Fairytale of New York' already out there and U2 the biggest band on earth, and Ireland beating England 1-0 — but slowly, the slovenly beast that is Official Ireland was starting to notice this and to endeavour to use it as best it could.

Around this time, you could hear the first furtive mentions of 'U2' in the Dáil chamber, perhaps validated by their appearance on the cover of *Time* magazine with the headline, 'Rock's Hottest Ticket', and the fact that they appeared to be making fantastic amounts of money, with aerial pictures of their grand houses in the papers — for Official Ireland, this was the clincher.

And inexorably, you would start to hear the odd mention of the Boys In Green and Jack Charlton on the official showcase of

Official Ireland, our old friend *Questions and Answers*. They would usually leave the 'sporty' topic until the end, the 'funny' question. And then, apparently summoning all his intellectual powers in order to read his own handwriting, a member of the audience would quote directly from the card he was holding in his trembling hand: 'Does the panel think … that Jack Charlton … the manager of the Republic of Ireland soccer squad … should be the next President of Ireland?'

Well, the laughing that would start …

———

But in 1987, the year that Ireland first qualified for a major tournament, Haughey did something that would forever change the nature of the discourse on *Q&A* and every other forum in which the official bullshit was spoken.

The 'tough decisions' he was taking are entirely debatable, but there is no doubt that he was an enthusiastic advocate of the International Financial Services Centre. Guided by the wisdom of his extraordinarily rich friends, Haughey was able to see that the IFSC could bring Paddy into a game he had never played with conspicuous success — the money game.

Haughey himself had been playing his own version of it for many years, byzantine in some ways, in other ways crudely simple — rich guys would just give him loads of money — but he could see how Paddy, in his off-shore way, might be well-placed to have a crack at the old 'financial services' industry and maybe even learn the language in the process.

Officially, it would go something like this: 'The IFSC was established under legislation designed to boost activity and employment in the Irish economy. The government had identified the growth potential of the international financial services sector and recognised that Ireland had the capacity to develop in the industry because of its well-developed financial infrastructure, a sophisticated national and international communications system, and a young and highly educated population.'

All good stuff there, but these things in themselves would not give Paddy the edge. The key to his success, in this new world, was the 'competitive corporate tax rate of 10%'. And what was described, with a perfectly straight face, as 'a sophisticated and responsive regulatory environment'.

Ah yes, a sophisticated and responsive regulatory environment.

We all know now that 'a sophisticated and responsive regulatory environment', when translated into English, means 'no regulatory environment at all'. It's the Wild West, baby! But back then, when the slums in the inner city were being levelled and the great towers of the IFSC were being constructed in their place, only members of the corporate class knew such things.

And there weren't many of them knocking around, at least not yet. Soon they would be everywhere, speaking sagely about our competitive corporate tax rate and our sophisticated and responsive regulatory environment, and soon they would involve themselves in the success story of Irish football as if they had, in fact, created it themselves.

But to give credit where it is due, when the Republic had nothing, when it needed the support of the big-swinging-mickey brigade, it was represented mainly by one man and one company. 'Put de boot in' would become a sort of national catchphrase, in imitation of Mr Arnold O'Byrne, then head of Opel, who became the official sponsors of the Republic before all the fine madness took hold — though it might be argued that having your brand-name inscribed on the shirts of the Republic at any time before 11 November 1987 was a form of madness in itself.

It was what we now call 'counter-intuitive', to have any commercial association with the FAI, yet through a series of remarkable events it turned out to be a truly great call by O'Byrne. And he was entitled to take all the credit for it, becoming the personification of the Opel brand in Ireland, appearing in all the TV ads himself.

He had this strange accent, rumoured to be a result of having spent time abroad, allied to a natural tendency to mix up his t's and th's, and the stiltedness that often comes when a TV amateur speaks for his own product. But all this just made him more endearing, and gave a distinctiveness to that killer line, 'put de boot in'. And Arnold had an actual product to sell, as distinct from a financial 'product'.

Soon the money-men would be buying into the success of the Republic, or perhaps just going to matches, ideally ones that were being played abroad in one of the great cities, in nice weather, but when it mattered, Arnold O'Byrne was out there, on his own.

In fact, the face of corporate Ireland in the 1980s manifested itself in just two men, Arnold O'Byrne and Maurice Pratt. Like Arnold, Maurice put himself in front of the people, doing the TV ads for Quinnsworth, and himself becoming something of a national figure or, if you like, a national joke.

Otherwise, one of our better-known entrepreneurs wasn't even a full-time businessman, at least not officially. Monsignor James Horan had orchestrated the building of Knock Airport which, like the DART, was regarded by many of the more respected economic commentators as a terrible waste of money and a monument to human folly.

Again, it was perhaps counter-intuitive to be building airports in a country which had a lot of people trying to get out of it, but very few trying to get back in, but Haughey gave it his blessing, for all sorts of reasons, not all of them good, not all of them bad.

One day in the late 1980s I found myself at Knock Airport in the middle of a scene which demonstrated the growing relationship between Irish business and Irish sport — though in these early stages, the relationship was still somewhat dysfunctional.

It was the day before Mayo played Cork in the 1989 All-Ireland final, and the Mayo squad had opted to get the plane to Dublin from Knock Airport instead of making the traditional train journey.

Which was all very sophisticated, except perhaps in the area of media management, because they insisted that no journalists be allowed on the flight itself — only photographers, who would take pictures of the lads at the airport as they boarded the plane and who would get the flight to Dublin with the team, if they needed it … and that would do.

Except that would not do the *Sunday Independent*, who summoned me to a crisis meeting, chaired by Editor Aengus Fanning and Sports Editor Adhamhnan O'Sullivan, and featuring what seemed to be the entire photographic staff of the Independent Group, in a very small, very hot room, in which various solutions were explored. This meeting resulted in an early start for me the following morning and a journey across the country with the photographer Jim O'Kelly (who is sadly no longer with us) with whom I would collaborate in a clandestine manoeuvre.

Jim would take the official snap of the lads at the airport, getting on the plane, but here was the clever bit: instead of him getting on the plane and bringing the film back to Dublin, he would quietly slip the roll of film to me, and then I, masquerading as a photographer, would get on the plane instead of him.

Jim would drive back to Dublin, his work done, while I would be enjoying the view of Ireland below and making notes for the exciting 'colour piece' I would write when I got back to the *Sunday Indo* offices with the precious film.

So it was that I spent several hours in Knock Airport pretending to be a photographer in order to establish some sort of authenticity for the moment when I would casually step aboard the plane, just another snapper. So it was that Jim gave me one of his cameras, which

I carried around for the day, pointing it at things in what I hoped was the style of a professional photographer — unfortunately, I may have aroused some suspicion among my fellow photographers, because, as I would eventually learn, for most of the day, the hood was covering the lens.

I pointed it anyway at the Mayo captain, Willie Joe Padden, and at T.J. Kilgallon and the rest of the lads as they arrived to continue the journey to Mayo's first All-Ireland final in 38 years. I followed them out onto the runway where RTÉ's finest were filming the ceremonial departure with commentary by Jimmy Magee, strenuously avoiding conversation with my colleagues, who all seemed to be very nice and anxious to welcome me to their dark trade with a few kind words. I continued to take pictures of the plane, of the players and of the crowds cheering behind the high wire fencing and of Jimmy Magee and indeed of anything that moved, or was about to move, as well as anything that was nailed down — all with the hood still covering the lens.

And when Jim had taken the actual picture, of the players standing on the steps of the plane, the 'switch' was done and apparently no-one was any the wiser. I boarded the plane, fooling them all — my face would not have been well-known in GAA circles, at the time — I took my seat near the back of the plane with my new-found photographic brethren, down there with the selectors, the mentors and various members of the county board, all oblivious to the stroke that had been pulled, and I got it done, more or less as had been planned in that hot little room the previous afternoon. I made the dash by taxi from Dublin Airport to Middle Abbey Street and wrote the piece which would appear in that Sunday's paper, which hit the streets on the Saturday night.

Mayo lost the match, by 0-17 to 1-11, which may be unrelated.

But the day's work on the whole prompts a few observations: on a personal note, it was another difficult situation for me at an airport in the company of an *Independent* photographer; and in general it demonstrates that in the run-up to Italia 90, Irish business and Irish sport were getting closer, without quite getting it right.

Clearly it was a coup for Knock Airport and the airline involved to have these iconic images out there, of the first Gaelic team to go to the All-Ireland on a plane — images that would be out there for all time, if Mayo had managed to win — but with their bizarre ban on journalists, they had managed to take the good out of it. They thought they were being smart, but they were only annoying us. If they'd been really smart, they could have had me or someone suitable 'fluffing' a piece by Willie Joe Padden about this remarkable event, with all the proceeds going into the 'pool' for some end-of-season trip to Los Angeles, or maybe Singapore.

The Boys In Green would become increasingly wise in these ways of the world, as Italia 90 loomed, but there was another party involved on that day in Knock, which would eventually get the hang of the art of self-promotion. Back then, that particular party could only do its best within the confines of what the GAA would allow.

I refer to the airline which brought us from Knock to Dublin in a plane which, as I recall, was named The Spirit of Connacht. It was just a modest outfit, and it was no surprise to see it operating out of an obscure venue such as Knock — in fact, I remember feeling a bit sorry that day for all involved in this struggling operation called Ryanair.

Nobody had heard at that time of Michael O'Leary, Ryanair's Chief Executive, we had only heard of Michael O'Leary, the socialist who had been a charismatic leader of the Labour Party. Indeed few had heard of any business leader except that man Arnold O'Byrne, who remains the only one of his kind who took a punt on Irish football before it went mega-platinum, not afterwards.

Afterwards, they were all heroes.

| THE BONO STORY

I think it's time that we called in Bono.

You may recall our living arrangements at that time, the basement flat in the old Geldof place in which I lived with Jane and the new-born Roseanne and the flat on the next floor occupied by Liam Mackey, the one that had the phone in the hall.

Jane and Roseanne and I went up there one day for coffee, just as Liam arrived along, accompanied by Bono.

Through all sorts of *Hot Press*-related contacts over the years, Liam had come to know Bono (a lot better than I did, to tell the truth) and on this occasion he had just bumped into him down the road in Dun Laoghaire. Now, I'm only telling you this because, by the late 1980s, most people in Ireland had sat down and chatted with Bono at some stage. So if we're trying to convey the spirit of that time, we should observe this formality. And there is a direct relevance to our project in the sense that U2, represented by Larry Mullen, had cranked up the build-up to Italia 90 with arguably the best football record ever made, 'Put 'Em Under Pressure'.

So it was a very Irish occasion, with Bono sitting there by the fireplace drinking his mug of coffee. He spoke movingly about the startling new direction in which the latest album was going (this would be *Achtung Baby*) before embarking on a series of anecdotes about various legends of Irish life and culture, especially in the showband realm.

In particular he recounted tales of a man called Jim Hand, one of the famous Hand twins from Drogheda, the other being Michael the journalist, a former Editor of the *Sunday Independent* — Michael indeed, got his start in journalism with *The Argus* newspaper in Dundalk, after a job interview for which Michael's place was actually taken by Jim, the interviewer being unaware that the wrong twin had turned up to fool him — or if he was aware, it didn't trouble him.

And though they would eventually conquer Dublin in their chosen fields of journalism and showbusiness, Jim would tell John Waters that he had never got on a bus in Dublin, 'because you'd never know where they'd be going' — an observation which, with the passing of time, seems wise in a Beckettian way.

Launching into an extraordinarily accurate rendition of the Drogheda accent, Bono shared his favourite Hand line, in which Jim Hand is introduced to someone at a social function and tells this person that he would very much like to get to know him because he seems like a very nice fellow, but that this is out of the question because unfortunately, he already knows enough people.

Bono told this story not in the superior tone of the rock star making fun of the boys of the old brigade, but with relish, admiring the fine clarity of Hand's vision, the originality of the statement. Psychologists may feel that Bono, here, was subconsciously identifying with Jim Hand because of his own desire not to have any more human relationships of a meaningful kind, having already reached his quota. And since the record shows that he still had about fifty million people left to meet and to empathise with between then and 2010, his current state of mind in this regard can only be imagined.

Interestingly, Larry Mullen's aforementioned 'Put 'Em Under Pressure (Olé Olé Olé)' also seemed to embrace the heroes of another time and to celebrate this interconnectedness by blasting off with the riff from 'Dearg Doom' by Horslips — you will recall that a member of that group, Eamon Carr, was present on that night that I agreed to write Paul McGrath's autobiography.

And to complete this great Celtic circle, Liam Mackey was also an indirect contributor to 'Put 'Em Under Pressure', because a filmed interview which he conducted with Big Jack was used on the record, supplying those rousing lines about going out there to compete, to put 'em under pressure.

Jack had been talking to Liam in an interview for a feature-length video called *Que Sera, Sera* made by Billy Magra, a manager of rock 'n' roll bands, a founding father of Irish stand-up comedy and later a TV producer. But Billy was a man ahead of his time in other ways. I remember an interview he did for *Hot Press* in which he said that one of the things he liked least about Ireland was the amount of private pain caused by alcohol. It was such a strange thing to read at the time from a creature of rock 'n' roll, that it stuck in my mind and has never gone away.

Ah, the fates are sending us these messages, but we do not receive them.

Billy's film, which I watched innumerable times while experiencing the private pain caused by alcohol, and which tells the story of how we got to Italia 90, was a brilliant piece of work. It captured all the rising fever of the campaign and the anticipation of what was to come.

As we prepared for Italia 90, it seemed as if so many strands of Irish culture were coming together, U2 allied with Horslips allied with Big Jack allied with many other worthy contributions in the national interest. And mercifully, the involvement of the rockers, as distinct from the usual old showbiz hacks, would mean that Ireland's ubiquitous anthem for the tournament, would actually be good.

'Put 'Em Under Pressure' was more than good, it was outstanding, it was powerful. There was 'Give It A Lash, Jack', by Liam Harrison and the GOAL celebrities, which actually wasn't bad at all. It had a thing almost unknown in the long and unhappy history of the football record, it had charm.

And The Pogues got involved too, with 'Jack's Heroes', accompanied by a video starring Tom Hickey, himself a seminal figure in Irish theatre and television drama: 'And the shout goes up / When the World Cup / Is raised on Stephen's Green', it went. And while it didn't quite establish itself in the hearts of the people, it confirmed our status as a nation with some gravitas. England could call on New Order and Keith Allen for their beguiling Italia 90 anthem 'World in Motion', and now here we were, with mere football songs being put together by the likes of U2 and Shane MacGowan, while these supposed aristos from Holland and Italy and Spain would be represented by … who? Certainly no-one from the top drawer, or even from the fourth or fifth drawer, probably some cabaret act trying to get himself noticed for next year's Eurovision. A sore point there, perhaps, because we ourselves had not yet risen above that particular weakness. And even in the fat years to come, we would gorge ourselves on several more Euro-romps, becoming serial winners of this thing, just because we could.

Poignantly, after the second or third time, one recalls a certain fear that took hold when it seemed certain that we would win another one and it was argued that RTÉ and the country in general just couldn't afford to keep going like this. The figure which frightened us so much was something like £1.5 million, which these days is not much more than the take-home pay of a couple of top RTÉ executives, but which was considered so onerous back then, it seemed to involve making a straight choice between hosting the Eurovision or cancelling all other TV programmes planned for that year.

We did it anyway, so anxious for recognition of any kind, we could not contemplate letting go of this weird knack that we had somehow mastered.

Money and the rise of the new nations of Eastern Europe would eventually free us from this need, but until then, Eurovision would embroil Paddy in many of the old familiar contradictions — even in his moment of celebration there would be a lingering pall of shame; even the thing he was good at was inherently bad.

But even this would have at least one unambiguously happy development, further on up the road — the director of the 1988 Eurovision, Declan Lowney, was a talented and ambitious chap and enough of a free spirit to complain openly to me in an interview for the *Sunday Independent* about some low-class act called Scott Fitzgerald that the Brits were sending over to represent them in the RDS. His outspokenness would have cost him a few extra moments of anxiety on the night, when the same Scott Fitzgerald was narrowly pipped for the top prize by the Swiss entry, sung by one Celine Dion.

In the 1988 show, Lowney had tried to do something genuinely different, replacing the usual half-time bullshit with a video of Hot House Flowers busking 'Don't Go' in cities all across Europe. The Flowers were supposed to become huge after this, as huge as Michael Flatley would become after a similar spectacular, but mysteriously, they didn't — too Irish, maybe. But Lowney would do the best work of all, leaving RTÉ to move to London and eventually becoming the director of *Ted*.

We were all trying to move beyond that Eurovision state of mind as we prepared ourselves for our debut on the vast, unforgiving stage that was Italia 90. And given the enthusiastic involvement of almost every element of Irish society, from the clowns of Official Ireland to the serious players of Killiney Hill, it seemed that we were looking at an unprecedented display of national unity.

————

Which, in many ways, we were.

Yet, after all these years I can still hear the voice of Father Michael Cleary coming through the wall.

Yes, there was always something there to remind us that the country, as they say, was not half-settled.

Needing a bit more space for child-rearing purposes, Jane and I and Roseanne had moved to an actual house on the other side of Dun Laoghaire, a very small terraced house, which of course we rented. And through the wall of that house every night, came the voice of Father Michael Cleary.

The old lady next door was hard of hearing, so she used to listen to his programme on 98FM with the volume turned up loud, this rambling show which sounded like an extended parish bulletin, frequently featuring members of Youth Defence and the voices of various other 'conservative' Catholic organisations. They had been on a war footing for most of the 1980s and had won some and lost some, and had nothing else to be doing for the foreseeable future.

So while we were presenting ourselves to the world as these wild and crazy guys who can go anywhere and enjoy the football and hold our drink, at home there was still a substantial minority who felt that a man such as Father Michael Cleary was a credible figure who still had something to contribute to the great debate.

Now that it's all over, it seems that the decline of the power of the Catholic Church in Ireland was some sort of an inevitable process, like the changing of the seasons, but in these pivotal years, the Church and its various storm-troopers were cocky after their victories in the abortion and divorce referenda and there was still a feeling that it could go either way.

Jane and I would feel the need to send Roseanne to a non-denominational school, something that wouldn't bother me greatly these days, but which at the time seemed like an issue that needed your full attention; Bishop Eamon Casey was still a prince of the church, much-loved and a gas character and most people were unaware that Father Michael Cleary was effectively a married man and a father in the biological sense.

Or at least they were unaware, up to a point.

Deep down, at some intuitive level, they must have known it. I don't exclude myself from this complex system of denial: I 'knew' that Cleary had a child, or children. Or at least I 'knew' that in the course of a lifetime doing what he did, in the way that he did it, it would be inconceivable that The Singing Priest did not have a child or children. I had this running joke with a friend who worked in a tabloid paper at the time, whereby I would always greet him with the words, 'Find Cleary's children', in the pompous tones of a Roman senator calling for Carthage to be destroyed. We 'knew' that there had to be at least one of them out there, but we also knew that it would be damnably hard to prove it. The aura of power still protected him, so that even a blackguard on the Father Michael Cleary scale seemed elusive, still free to roam.

Yet he was a more fantastic creation than we had imagined at the time. Until Italia 90, perhaps the greatest single gathering of people on the island of Ireland in the latter part of the 20th century was for the visit of Pope John Paul II in 1979, and Cleary had been the master of ceremonies.

He was there on the stage in Galway with Bishop Eamon Casey, getting the crowd going in that vast arena as if he was working the room at the Old Shieling.

We often hear commentators musing on the way that sport has replaced religion as the great communal activity of our time, except usually they are lamenting this, seeing it as an example of how we have lost our way. Perhaps they should reflect further on this in the case of Ireland, where the Pope's visit would be followed by a decade of want, while the Charlton years would be followed by a decade of plenty. Perhaps they should reflect further on this, as they recall that the cheerleaders for the Pope would turn out to be deeply disturbed individuals while Charlton would never lose the respect and the gratitude of the people. And perhaps they should reflect even further on this, as they observe that we no longer felt the need to be supervised by priests and religious on our feast days. That we had surely grown up just a little, when we had Bill O'Herlihy up there as the chief moderator and John Giles and Eamon Dunphy getting us up for it, instead of Cleary and Casey — if that is not progress …

———

I have already alluded to the fact that I lived across the road from this Father Michael Cleary for a while. For about two years, indeed, I lived in a flat in Leinster Road in Rathmines (didn't we all?) and Father Mick lived in a house on the other side of the road, maybe fifty yards away.

Another *Hot Press* contributor, Michael O'Higgins, was also living in the neighbourhood, in a flat that was actually smaller than my own, from which he would emerge to join me for a late pint in the Leinster Inn, both of us entirely unaware of the true nature of Father Mick's living arrangements — nor indeed would Father Mick have been aware that his daily movements were being observed by fellows from that well-known anti-God magazine.

Mick O'Higgins, back then, was more exercised by various other blackguards in our midst, conducting interviews with the likes of Christy Dunne and Martin Cahill, all of which doubtless prepared him for his eventual career as one of the country's best criminal lawyers and one of the few Senior Counsel who has spent any meaningful amount of time on the inside of a Rathmines bedsitter. Yet even O'Higgins' forensic skills didn't crack open the truth about the lifestyle of Father Michael Cleary.

I would see him all the time, coming out of that house and getting into his car engulfed in smoke from the cigarettes that he smoked incessantly.

I 'knew' that he was a man with normal urges which I 'knew' that he indulged the same as any other man, yet it somehow never occurred to me for a moment that he might be indulging them behind the door of that house from which he emerged every day. That he would be out there performing his pastoral duties, whatever they might be, or broadcasting his rigidly orthodox Catholic opinions to the people of Dublin from the studios of 98FM, at the end of which he went home and went to bed. With his wife.

Like all the best chancers, the true professionals, he had been hiding in plain sight. And he got away with it.

He was dead by the time that his 'wife', Phyllis Hamilton, told the story of their relationship, which was not entirely unlike any other long-term relationship between a man and a woman, except for the fact that she was pretending to be his housekeeper and he was pretending to be a celibate Roman Catholic priest. Their son, Ross, was just trying to be himself against these almost insurmountable odds.

But others must have 'known' about it, with or without the inverted commas. There were various characters that Cleary would bring home with him for late-night games of poker, with refreshments provided by his loyal housekeeper, which gave rise to one of the outstanding lines of the story, with Cleary telling the lads to throw 'a few quid into the pot for poor oul Phyllis'.

It would be nearly twenty years until the emergence of a sort of home movie of life behind the door of that house, a documentary called *At Home With The Clearys*, made by film-maker Alison Millar, who during her student days had shot a few apparently innocuous domestic scenes of Father Mick and his 'housekeeper' Phyllis and her son Ross. It is an amazing film, featuring this video diary of what we now realise was a secret family. It was made with the co-operation of Ross, and all the more powerful because it is not unkind to Cleary. It tries to show why the poor folks of Ballyfermot and Ballymun were so in thrall to him — basically, he was all they had, the only representative of Official Ireland who paid any attention to them. It showed that he had a certain generosity of spirit, a largeness of character, of that there is no doubt.

Given his privileged background, it was clear that he could have had a perfectly normal life gambling and golfing and whoring without all the priestly bits thrown in. But he wanted it all. And I suspect that his background also partly explains why he thought he could get away with it: he was a member of that ruling class in Ireland, which had run the place since the foundation of the state, assiduously maintaining all the advantages for themselves and keeping everyone else in their place.

For example, he would be 'looking after' unmarried mothers, quietly passing their children on to deserving middle-class couples, or just keeping tabs on them.

In this role he saw abortion as the greatest of all evils — perhaps the only evil — to be conquered using all the skills at his disposal. These skills included his empathy for people who were in deep trouble, his ability to give them a bit of hope with a story or a song, and his almost unquantifiable reserves of complete and absolute bullshit.

Ah, he was a disgraceful man, in so many ways. And yet, in saying that, I realise that he brings out things in me that I don't like in myself. I don't like to be judging people, and I don't like people judging me.

Which probably helps to explain the ferocity and the longevity of this battle between what you might call the old-fashioned values of 'rural Ireland' and what is termed the liberal agenda of 'Dublin 4'.

I don't care for these terms any more as years of over-use by some of the more cynical characters in Irish life have rendered them virtually meaningless, but at this time of which we speak, there was a black-and-white split between these rival forces, made all the more horrible by this mutual ability to bring out the worst in each other.

Charlie McCreevy, lionised by many a *Questions and Answers* panellist for his supposedly brilliant sense of humour, said something amusing once about his own constituency of Kildare, in which Allenwood was perhaps the quietest and the most nondescript of all the quiet and nondescript villages in the county — 'And even in Allenwood, there is a Dublin 4 set'.

Dublin 4 is a state of mind which most of us like to think is essentially un-Irish, this tendency to be ashamed of our own past and our own people, as unforgiving as the old ways which were under attack.

And it is a state of mind, too, which lacks a genuine appreciation of the way things really worked, how it might actually be a good thing to cover up a little local scandal, how it could be a great kindness to hide the truth with a load of bullshit. Or, if you like, with 'a sophisticated and responsive regulatory environment'.

Yes, for generations before the establishment of the IFSC, Paddy had been running a sophisticated and responsive regulatory environment all over the place, in ways that the supposed sophisticates of the new Ireland of the 1980s didn't entirely grasp. But somehow in the 1980s it started to shift from the usual nonsense about farmers paying tax, to something else altogether.

At its most harmless, it manifested itself in the 'moving statues', which always gets a bit of an indulgent chuckle from the sages of Official Ireland, a form of localised voodoo which was also frowned upon by Official Catholic Ireland, including at least one bishop who was reprimanded by Eamonn McCann with these lines: 'Here is a man, who, on a daily basis, purports to transform quantities of bread and wine into the body and blood of a person who allegedly lived about 2,000 years ago. I think he has a cheek'.

I quoted this line in a piece for the *Sunday Independent*, leading to an odd little scene which demonstrated that Official Ireland might be pooh-poohing this as 'silly season stuff', yet it could have echoes of something deeper.

I was stopped in the corridor of the *Independent* a few days after my piece was published by Sean Ryan, the football writer, who started to talk about my use of that quote of McCann's. Sean is a nice man, so there was nothing menacing in his approach, but he was adamant that by quoting this paragraph of McCann's, I had been appallingly offensive to many readers who were practising Catholics.

At first I thought he was referring to McCann's criticism of the bishop, but he insisted that that wasn't a problem, that bishops are only human and can be criticised just like anyone else. No, his problem was that the Eucharist — which is essential to the Liturgy — was being disrespected here.

I hardly knew Sean at all, so I had no idea about his religious beliefs, but this wasn't the only reason why I found it hard to get my head around this encounter. Again, like the time I was accused of blasphemy by Bishop Comiskey, in a much more public fashion, it had never crossed my mind that such a reaction would be forth-coming — I wasn't actually trying to be offensive, which sort of took the good out of it for me — but Sean and I stood there anyway, like creatures from a different solar system, meeting for the first time.

And I suppose what made it bamboozling for me was the question that formed in my mind: would the people out there ever believe that in a corridor of Independent House, two men from the *Sunday Independent* were having a sincere and intense discussion about the role of transubstantiation in the context of the Liturgy? I don't think so. Yet there was a civility about this encounter, which would not be apparent in the darker conflicts of that time.

And Sean being a football man was a help.

———

Looking back on the many accomplishments of Jack and the lads, I can think of no other force which came close to creating a sense that

Irish people were generally embarked on a common purpose. In every other significant area of national life, you couldn't go far without encountering this cultural split between the old Ireland and the emerging one. In fact, there can be no doubt that this fracture in the national psyche contributed greatly to all the other failures we were experiencing — if Ireland in the 1980s was a person, it would be described as 'dysfunctional', self-destructive, tormented by these incompatible ideas about how we should live.

And the only thing which could apparently make it better was this sense of belonging to the alternative Republic of Ireland, a better place, ruled by the benign dictator, Jack. From Euro 88 onwards, as the big matches got bigger, it felt like everyone was on the same side for a change. I have this abiding image of a nun driving her little car a bit faster than usual down the Stillorgan dual carriageway to get home in time for a game of which she probably knew nothing except that it was very, very important for Ireland to win. Or maybe to draw. If he did nothing else, Jack Charlton could claim that he made the Irish feel like they all lived in the same country for a while.

And, in time, we got the idea that it was better for us to be living like this than to be going back to the two-nations approach, where typically something terrible would happen in rural Ireland — the death in 1984 of 15-year-old Ann Lovett and the infant to which she gave birth in the grotto in Granard would be the most terrible example — and the Dublin media would arrive in large numbers to find out The Truth. The locals would suddenly be transformed into the cast of *Bad Day At Black Rock*, sullen and secretive and hostile, convinced that every reporter was Spencer Tracy, trying to find out their awful secret. And of course they were not entirely wrong.

Deep down, the majority of journalists were convinced that they were dealing with a crowd of incorrigible rogues who were congenitally dishonest and mired in obscurantism. And of course they were not entirely wrong.

And yet being right about so much does not necessarily mean that you will always be doing the right thing. I, for one, was not living a life markedly more righteous than Father Michael Cleary's. I was drinking a lot, whereas Cleary didn't drink at all. I was smoking nearly as much as he was; I was gambling nearly as much; for all I know, I was not even as good a 'husband' as he was, though I did acknowledge my own child. I was not offering succour to people in distress, as he was, and if I had a nightly radio show, I would not have been reading out requests from prisoners in Wheatfield, as he did all the time.

In my defence, I would say that I was not presenting myself to the world as a celibate Catholic priest, as he was.

Ah, he wanted it all. He wanted it every way, but he could not have kept that schtick going for so long if he hadn't been striking a few resonant chords with the people of Ireland — the major chords always followed by the minor chords; the little moments of apparent joy always followed by the shafts of remorse.

I say 'apparent' joy, because in Cleary we can see something of what Evelyn Waugh meant when he described the Irish as a joyless people — this might seem like a strange observation on the face of it, given the way that we present ourselves to the world, yet while Waugh was no friend of the Irish, that doesn't mean he was wrong. Cleary would tend to give that line of Waugh's some credibility. There was no real joy in him — he was too much of a control freak for that.

In fact, it was not until the arrival of Bono that we found ourselves a real singing priest, who could do joy, who could be standing on stage in Croke Park singing about pride in the name of love with nothing to be ashamed about and God on his side.

We have always done sadness superbly, but Bono is the first Irish artist of renown who has made it his business to generate these sensations of joy and he has spoken of how hard it is to convey this thing called joy — it must be harder still, given the bit of Paddy in him.

It is another of our little contradictions, this impression we give to the world that we are bursting with merriment when in fact we are wasting away with melancholia. Which makes our journey with Jack all the more meaningful — because it is arguable that Italia 90 and everything surrounding it was the most sustained period of joy in the entire history of the people of Ireland. And some day we might even manage to do it again, only sober this time.

Now that the war is long over — and his side lost the decisive battle by a terrifyingly thin margin in the Divorce Referendum of 1995 — I suspect that we would feel most comfortable with the story of Father Michael Cleary rendered as a musical comedy. We would prefer the broad strokes, the holy man warming up the crowd at Knock for the Pope along with Bishop Eamon Casey and the hilarious twist, whereby he would later tell Casey about his son Ross, but he would have to find out about Casey's son from the hated media.

The Singing Priest! it would of course be called, a madcap romp through the playing fields of the GAA where he first got the thirst for glory, to the austere manly world of the seminary and on to stardom as the peoples' priest who could sing a song and tell a joke about God, and who was loved by the ladies … and the rest of it kinda writes itself, as they say.

We would prefer to experience the life and times of Father Mick again as musical theatre, because human beings can't take too much reality, and Paddy can probably take less of it than most.

We were preparing to abandon it altogether in this glorious time called Italia 90.

Chapter 10 ∽

| SUMMER NIGHTS

Jack Charlton was perhaps the one man in the world who had less belief that Ireland could win the World Cup than we had ourselves.

In fact, like most of us, I doubt if the thought ever entered his head. But he had a belief that the Irish could play in the World Cup and not disgrace themselves and when Jack genuinely believed something, he would usually find a way to get it done.

Even now, one can but marvel at how the Irish found Jack, and Jack found the Irish. He hadn't even wanted the job, at least not much. He could take it or leave it, which gave him a certain lightness of being which he would not have had in the England job, one which he genuinely wanted. But he would have been a very bad manager of England because they have this crazy belief that they can win the World Cup and they expect the manager to deliver on what they regard as a perfectly reasonable expectation.

Jack, no more than Ron Greenwood, or Don Revie, or Bobby Robson, or Graham Taylor, or Glen Hoddle, or Kevin Keegan, or Terry Venables, or Steve McLaren, or Sven, could not have fulfilled that expectation. And it would have been a very ugly scene.

But somehow, he found himself managing the Irish, who had been conditioned to adopt an attitude which to him came naturally — above all else, the object of the exercise is to avoid disgracing yourself.

They say that Jack was always like that, that he had a sense of when the job was done, which was not often shared by his more ambitious colleagues. Even at Leeds Utd, who were in the running for every major title in England and Europe for several years, Jack could be heard wondering aloud how the fuck they kept getting themselves into these situations. You would normally hear a player talking like that on the last day of the season as his team of perennial strugglers faced into another match which they needed to win to avoid relegation. But Jack would be cursing Leeds' incorrigible habit of getting themselves into situations when they needed a result to win the League, or maybe even the Double. 'How do we do it?' he would say, shaking his head sadly.

Which might feed into that Official Ireland cliché of the Gruff Yorkshireman, except it wasn't quite as simple as that.

Jack was regarded by his teammates, not least John Giles, as a top-class player. He also had qualities of honesty and decency, which would far out-weigh these curmudgeonly aspects. And he was a deceptively skilful player of the media game. He raised no objections to the conventional wisdom that he had taken over the football team of this small country, with players of limited ability, and that the Irish were punching above their weight. And this wasn't just the conventional wisdom of the hounds of Wapping: it was put about so much, most of the Irish believed it, too.

————

Drawn against England again in the first round of Italia 90, we now had one overriding need, which was the same overriding need we had had in Euro 88: above all else, the object of the exercise was to avoid disgracing ourselves. In a perverse way, the fact that we were drawn in the same group as England again would have suited Jack. It concentrated the mind on something other than winning the World Cup. That was for others, such as Italy, and Germany, and Argentina and … ahem … England.

In fact, our thoughts were still so far away from such extravagant notions, it ensured a perfect meeting of minds between the manager and the multitudes. We were also up against Wor Dutch again, a wearying thought for both us and them, but Egypt, the fourth team in the Group, represented the road to freedom.

In our own way we had an imperialist attitude to Egypt, knowing little about them but sort of assuming that we would always be better than them at football. Just by some process of natural selection. Since the four best third-placed teams would qualify from the six Groups, the deal went something like this: we would do everything humanly possible against England to avoid being disgraced; we would probably struggle against Holland but so would everyone else, so we didn't mind that; and since Holland would beat Egypt, and England would probably beat Egypt too, it surely wouldn't be beyond our capabilities to do slightly better than Egypt. And thus the job would be done. And Ireland would be free.

Again, one can but wonder what Jack wanted from this World Cup, in which four of the six Groups would send three teams to the last 16, making the task of qualifying from the Group stage about as easy as it gets, if that's all you want. And I really do believe that's all Jack wanted, but in matching our limited ambitions, Jack also gave leadership. He may have been the one man in the world who had less belief that Ireland could win the World Cup than we had ourselves, but he strongly believed that we could get a result against England. Or even against Wor Dutch. And he was able to communicate that belief.

He had worked it out.

He kept talking about having gone to the last World Cup and taken notes, which told him that every country was playing the same way, with this slow-build-up and a lot of passing the ball back and forth across the field to no apparent purpose. He saw that there was a place for something a lot more, shall we say, uncomplicated. In fact, it was his great strength and his great weakness, that he could only see the game, and indeed the world, through his own eyes.

And those were the eyes of a big centre-half. A very good, big centre-half, but one who believed that if he received the ball on the edge of his own penalty area, there was a fair chance he might lose it, so as a player he would try to avoid that, and as a manager he would insist, on pain of death, that anyone playing for him would avoid it, too.

It was not an attractive message, but there was something very attractive in the absolute clarity with which he expressed it. There was never a sliver of doubt in the minds of the players as to what was expected of them. And that if they failed to do it, they were gone. Even if they were Liam Brady, late of Juventus, they were gone.

Though Jack would claim that he was not just an unthinking philistine who had something against creative players, *per se* — he would find a place for his own brother, Bobby, in any team that he managed, because Bobby was, after all, perhaps the greatest footballer who ever lived. Yes, he would always pick Bobby — BUT ONLY IF HE DID WHAT JACK WANTED HIM TO DO.

Several of the Irish players could do a lot more than what Jack wanted them to do, but even they responded to this quality of leadership in him, helped by the fact that it seemed to be working and getting them to places they'd never been before in a green shirt.

And the people responded too.

Historically, Paddy was not unfamiliar with the tongue of the Englishman issuing crude instructions and expecting total obedience. But in this case, he seemed to be doing rather well out of it.

And there was a certain feeling of liberation too, a sense that we had been freed from all that bullshit of ours about the great poets and the great patriots and the great saints. Now all we wanted was what any other normal people wanted — a result.

We appreciated the fact that Jack seemed to insist on doing things properly, things we mightn't do quite as properly ourselves with our fetish for improvisation, for busking it. Things that the FAI could never have done without expert help, like bringing the players to Malta before the World Cup, to acclimatise. Watching the players sunning themselves over there in Malta, we felt a strange sense of ownership, almost a sense that they were members of our own family who had done well for themselves, stretched out there beside the pool getting a tan.

Could we afford this? Of course we could, we were in the World Cup now, and it was a long way from that poor sick scribe slumped across the typewriter in his darkened hotel room in Malta, a long way from his desolate words: 'Last night in the Ta' Qali …'

But we were on a mission as well as a holiday, because we would not just be facing England, we would be facing the England supporters, who still had a reputation as the worst hooligans on the face of the earth. We would be sent down there to Cagliari, on the island of Sardinia, we, the best supporters in the world, thrown in with this horde of nazi bastards. And then over to Sicily for the next two matches, more frigging hardship, more frigging boats, more planning to be done. And planning was never our strong suit.

It was as if they were trying to load all these logistics onto Paddy so that he simply wouldn't have the time or the energy to get drunk and to engage the enemy. We, the good guys, would be shipped off the mainland to provide opposition for these low-lifes. We would be put in cages, just like them. To protect us from them.

The Dutch, we imagined, would be too stoned to be getting stuck in or involved in any coherent way, and the Egyptian fans probably wouldn't bother coming at all.

Again, our theory of Irish exceptionalism hadn't quite worked out as we supposed it might. Could FIFA not have quietly arranged it so that we'd be drawn against Italy, in Rome, which would suit us in so many ways, culturally, historically and indeed alcoholically? And suit Italy too, because obviously they'd beat us?

Ah, but perhaps we had been chosen for a higher task. Like the monks of the Blaskets, it would fall to us to keep the flame of civilisation alive down there on the island. We would wear our colours, not just to express our pride in our lads, but to distinguish ourselves from the English and to say, 'We are not them'.

It appealed to Paddy's innate sense of martyrdom, this idea that we would stand for goodness, even for Christianity, against the heathens — a bit like the way that Archbishop McQuaid wanted the football men of Dublin to stand against the Communists — except this time we'd do it. Like we had done throughout the ages. And we would do it with great big smiles plastered all over our faces, because we would be drinking our heads off, just like the enemy, except we would not go mad, like them, and kill a load of innocent people. We would go mad in a good way.

And there were some other matches going on as well.

It was lovely feeling, to be sitting in the International on a bright Friday afternoon, drinking pints of Guinness and watching the opening match of the World Cup, knowing that we were actually involved in this thing. That these great events — even the opening ceremony — concerned us in some tangible way. That we no longer had our noses pressed up against the window, watching the feasting within.

I had felt this same sense of belonging, as a child, on the day in 1970 that Athlone Town played their first match in the League of Ireland against Shamrock Rovers. It was almost too much to take in, this move to higher ground, where you would encounter beings you knew only by reputation, wondrous mythical creatures like Mick Leech and Frank O'Neill and all the other class acts who played for Rovers at that time. And there were feelings of danger too — these guys could destroy you in five seconds if you weren't careful.

Embarrassment would duly come in a big way. It would be seen all over the football world in TV pictures showing the Athlone keeper swinging from the crossbar and breaking it during the FAI Cup semi-final against Finn Harps — breaking it twice indeed, for the punchline. Oh, how they laughed.

But I felt that sense of belonging again when the Town moved to even higher ground, on the day they played AC Milan in St Mel's Park in the UEFA Cup in 1975, the match that famously ended in a scoreless draw with John Minnock, Athlone's best player, missing a penalty.

Over the years I have become a sort of unofficial historian of that seminal event, a story which I think draws its terrible power from the strange magnificence of that missed penalty — the trauma of it, the sheer mad profligacy of it, the absurd waste of such an opportunity to defeat these gods who had brought their own food and wine to this remote place at the end of the world, and who had watched in awe as a pipe band marched around the pitch before kick-off, led by a goat.

And apart from the superstar, Gianni Rivera, and Albertosi, the Italy goalkeeper in the 1970 World Cup Final against Brazil, who saved Minnock's penalty, and the hatchet-man, Romeo Benetti, one of the Milanese who witnessed this was a former player who had just joined their coaching staff, a chap called Giovanni Trapattoni.

The missing of that penalty created a sort of magic which neither side could find the energy to disturb for the rest of that game, and for about an hour of the return match in the San Siro stadium. I now have no doubt, having reflected deeply on this, that if John Minnock had scored that penalty, Milan would have had their arrogance pricked enough to get mad and to get even, and possibly to beat us out the door.

And it would all have been forgotten.

Instead it was all coming back to me, in all its raging glory, as George Byrne and I and a full house of Friday-afternoon boozers watched Argentina playing Cameroon in the first match of Italia 90, knowing that on Monday night it would be our turn, against the old enemy, England.

The opening match was held in Milan, in the San Siro where the Town had held out for 63 minutes until AC put them away with three goals.

And there was madness in Cameroon, too.

There is always madness in places like Cameroon when they get a big result and we read a little paragraph in the paper quietly informing us that 23 people were killed in various stampedes and shooting incidents as fans celebrated on the streets for a fortnight.

We sort of envied them for their utter lack of inhibition and the fact that they had something to celebrate, regardless of the health and safety aspects. And now they were beating Argentina, the holders.

They had been playing in defiance of all the stereotypes. They weren't going to be kicked back home to Africa by the Argie strongmen, leaving Maradona to destroy what was left of them. It was they who were doing the kicking and getting two red cards for it. And they could play a bit, too. Cameroon won 1-0, which had to be a good thing for us.

Anything which seemed to upset the natural order, boded well.

The saps were rising.

The BBC had picked 'Nessun Dorma' as its signature tune for Italia 90, a stroke of executive genius which would be almost unimaginable in the BBC of today.

You would hear it said by its detractors that for decades, the BBC tended to be over-staffed with cravat-wearing characters who had one decent idea back in 1968 and then popped out for a drink, and hadn't been seen in the office since. Mind you, that one idea would have been something like … 'What about sending old Attenborough up the jungle for a while, and seeing what happens?' Or, 'As regards Association Football, say, an hour of highlights on Saturday night when the working classes have relaxed themselves with a few ales?' The idea of having Pavarotti singing 'Nessun Dorma' as the theme song for Italia 90 could only have come from that BBC tradition of

leisurely enlightenment. Perhaps with a touch of alcoholic enlightenment on the side.

In retrospect, we can see that it was perhaps the last hurrah of that
tradition, before the Corporation became inhabited by smaller
minds and smaller men. Today it would be argued that the song is
too upmarket or that the young people couldn't relate to it, or there's
nothing in it for women, or some such bollocks.

Of course it captivated viewers from the start and sent Pavarotti to
Number 2 in the UK charts ('World in Motion' was at Number 1). And
more than this, it gave the impression that it was Pavarotti who had
caught a break here, that his art was being honoured by its association
with the great art of football, and not the other way round — an
impression which Pavarotti, to his credit, appeared to endorse.

So the BBC opening sequence had the fat man singing, along with
pictures of the opera and of nymphettes dancing around the globe
and then the true art, images of Pele punching the air to celebrate his
goal in the World Cup Final in 1970, and of Johan Cruyff giving
some unfortunate full-back twisted blood, and of Maradona
hurdling a tackle, and ... and there's Ronnie Whelan, after scoring
against the USSR.

We were there, appearing in the same movie as those guys. It had
been confirmed by the BBC itself.

The sequence finished with the famous celebration by Marco
Tardelli, scorer of the third goal for Italy in their 3-1 win over
Germany in the Final of 1982. Running towards the touchline, his
arms spread wide, shaking his head from side to side as if to savour
all the incandescence of the moment, he is a vision of male ecstasy
out of the Renaissance. The same Tardelli is now Assistant Manager
of the Republic of Ireland.

Des Lynam was the BBC anchorman, still representing its urbane
traditions in his own way, before he moved to ITV and — as always
happened by some mysterious law of TV nature — lost his aura

overnight by the mere fact of moving from the Corporation to the 'commercial' outfit.

The fever was upon us now.

Italy beat Austria 1-0 in the Stadio Olimpico on the Saturday night, generating an atmosphere in Rome which they would try to maintain throughout the tournament, a succession of luminous football nights which would convince the world that all World Cups should be held in Italy.

We did not need any convincing.

The winning goal was scored late in the game by the substitute, one Salvatore (Totò) Schillaci. He had not started the game, yet he looked like a star, with all these stereotypical Italian qualities of *brio* and *braggadoccio*.

And we were playing in this thing, on Monday.

We kept hearing of men who, swept away with the excitement, abandoned all their responsibilities and borrowed money under false pretences from the Credit Union to go to Italy. And it was always the Credit Union, not American Express or Mastercard — Paddy had yet to discover the magic of plastic. One can only surmise that the Credit Unions of Ireland at the time were staffed with unworldly people, who were unable to make the connection between this wave of borrowing and the amount of money a man might need to get to Italy and to drink wildly for about ten days. And perhaps even to come back.

We learned something then, about the extent of the black economy. And about the resourcefulness of the people when their country needed them.

In Roddy Doyle's novel *The Van*, the unemployed Jimmy Rabbitte Snr and his best friend Bimbo become entrepreneurs during Italia 90, when Bimbo buys a broken-down chip van. There would be a great demand for fish and chips and batterburgers and chips and spice burgers and chips and breast of chicken and chips and curry sauce at this time. And Italia 90 would be a constant source of drunken banter with all the Italian-Irish chip-shop proprietors.

People who had no money, found money. They would sell a leather jacket. They would bring a bunch of albums to Freebird Records on Grafton Street or to the Basement Record and Tape Exchange on Bachelors Walk. They would sell a tumble drier or a cow.

But there was also a growing belief at home that if you went to Italy for the World Cup, you might miss it.

Chapter 11 ～

| EUPHORIC RECALL

We got it into our heads that there should be a buffet, with cold cuts.

This being the occasion of Ireland's first ever appearance in the World Cup, we felt that something special was needed, some gesture on our part, some effort to eat. Maybe we were trying to maintain a façade of civilisation in an increasingly primitive environment, but we probably just liked saying 'cold cuts', after hearing it in some movie. And it sounded a bit more Mediterranean than ham. Given the intensity of the night's promise, it had a pleasantly ludicrous ring to it: 'cold cuts'.

The plan was, Arthur Mathews and I would go to Liam's flat, the old place on Crosthwaite Park, and there we would partake of cold cuts, but mostly of cold beer and then we would watch whatever awaited us down there in Cagliari. Which we guessed might remove any appetite we had for cold cuts, for ham, salami, chorizo, German sausage, or food of any kind.

We guessed right.

But to prepare our palates for it, Arthur and I began the build-up in the Purty Kitchen in Dun Laoghaire, where the afternoon match was being shown on the television — the big screen was up on the next floor, awaiting the evening crowd.

The afternoon match was Scotland v Costa Rica, which we suspected might provide us with just about the perfect pre-match entertainment, and which didn't disappoint us in any way. In fact,

Scotland exceeded all our expectations by losing 0-1 to Costa Rica, a result that would help Costa Rica into the last 16. It was such a comfort to know that whatever happened to us in Cagliari, there was always someone worse off than us, a nation of chronically unfortunate men who would be doomed forever to watch their team doing things like this, losing to Costa Rica and then beating Holland, or maybe Brazil, but too late to do them any good. Or scoring a late winner in Bulgaria to put someone else through.

The Fear was growing inside of us, but the combination of the drink and the Scots was helping us to cope. We loved those guys, for what they were giving us — a comic opera that had been running forever, and that will never close.

But we didn't want to be joining them in it, on this night.

We were sick with The Fear as we walked to the other side of Dun Laoghaire to partake of the buffet. Or not as the case may be.

It was an admirable spread, in many ways, and many compliments were given to Liam but I can't recall actually eating any of it. I was growing increasingly disillusioned with eating in general, at the time. Though I noted that Liam had added a bowl of these things called cherry tomatoes, which were only starting to become popular in Ireland at that time — he confessed that the aspect of the cherry tomato which most appealed to him was that it required no cooking of any kind, to be enjoyed. The celebrity chef had yet to become a significant figure in our society.

———

RTÉ didn't have 'Nessun Dorma' but they were getting a feel for the ferocity of the people's passion.

Football men have always said that the litmus test of football's true popularity in Ireland is when GAA fixtures are cancelled because they clash with a big football match. Now concerts in Dublin by the likes of Mick Jagger and Prince were being cancelled, and RTÉ seemed to 'get' it, capturing the country's mania for football by filming school kids all over the country, singing 'Give It A Lash, Jack' and 'Olé Olé Olé'. For those of us who had sat in the International that day, waiting for Bulgaria to beat Scotland, or who had heard Éamonn MacThomáis declaring that Brian Boru was the only fella who could beat them Danes, this was a charming development. But we knew that the little ones couldn't possibly understand the true gravity of the situation, as we watched them singing their songs with just a few minutes to go until kick-off.

Down at the RDS, a huge crowd was watching it on a suitably huge screen, and drinking a lot of lager. There was no doubt now that this was the biggest communal event since the visit of the Pope, or perhaps even the Eucharistic Congress of 1932, except now we had this thing called free will.

And the Leaving Cert was starting the following day. A few hundred yards away from Crosthwaite Park, Dion Fanning was watching Giles and Dunphy making their closing remarks, knowing that whatever the outcome, he would be going to an exam hall the following day for the first English paper, no doubt quipping good-naturedly that if he wasn't defeated by the English this evening, he would certainly be defeated in the morning.

Fanning, who last appeared in our narrative as a nine-year-old tearing up that picture of the hated referee Nazare, is now a friend and a colleague of Liam Mackey's in the press box. But on the opening night of Italia 90 he had an even heavier burden to carry than the rest of us — on the morning after, no-one was going to ask us to discuss the character of Othello or to furnish written evidence that we had been reading *Pride and Prejudice* in the approved fashion. *Juno and the Paycock* was also on that year, though there is probably a tad more pleasure to be had getting drunk with the cast on Broadway, than composing an essay on O'Casey's use of Hiberno-English in an exam hall.

Yes, there is always someone worse off than yourself.

But it didn't feel like that when Gary Lineker scored for England after only eight minutes, somehow knocking a cross from Chris Waddle past Packie and finishing it with himself and Mick McCarthy in a heap in the net.

That was the coldest cut of all.

It was a horrible goal, scored in horrible weather, rain and thunder which we originally thought would have no effect on us: conditions were not good for football, but since we knew that Ireland had no intention of playing football anyway, we thought that if anything this would be to our advantage.

Now, it just reinforced our grief, thinking of how it would surely crush the spirits of the lads on the park and of course our brethren behind the cages on the terraces who had gone to Cagliari to show their Christian goodness and superiority to the 'ooligans. And who, we imagined, would now have had to listen to their hideous triumphalism, their cries of 'No Surrender to the IRA' and other finely crafted satirical barbs.

And yet when that goal went in, there was what Norman Mailer has called the strange sense of relief you feel when everything has turned to total catastrophe. Once the thing that is giving you The Fear has happened, and happened so soon, you know at least that you need no longer fear it.

But it didn't look good.

We could no longer cheat reality, as we had cheated it in Stuttgart. Packie couldn't keep the English out forever, and the ugliness of the goal seemed to suggest that the baleful gods were giving them something back for the miseries of Euro 88.

If there was any luck going around we felt it was the Irish that needed it, not an England team with John Barnes and Lineker and

Gazza himself. So when the gods started doling it out to Gary Lineker, giving him perhaps the only goal of his career which he effectively chested into the net from several yards out, we wondered just how ugly this was going to get. And we knew we needed to score, at least once. Which confronted us with one of the more painful realities of Jack's system, the fact that it wasn't really about us scoring, it was about the other team not scoring.

High on the improbability of it all, we had been making the best of it and celebrating this idea of putting 'em under pressure, celebrating it indeed with a full studio production by Larry Mullen Junior. But even the lager-maddened throng at the RDS could not entirely escape the reality that some day we might need a goal, very badly. And that the best of way of scoring a goal, usually, is by playing something that resembles football.

Which we did not do.

It can even be argued that Jack invented a new code, a sort of Compromise Rules game which perfectly combined aspects of Gaelic football with a smattering of Association Football, again demonstrating Jack's almost spooky compatibility with Paddy, how two dreams met. Aided by the back-pass rule which, in 1990, still allowed the ball to be kicked back to the keeper and the keeper to pick it up with his hands and to kick it up the park at his leisure, just like a Gaelic player, Jack had absolutely no problem with the notion that Packie Bonner might be our 'playmaker' — receiving the ball from the defenders and booting it as far away from his own goal as possible, hopefully towards an Irish player. But that wasn't important — as long as it was up the other end, according to Jack, the other crowd wouldn't be scoring.

But how were we to score?

Just as Jack's brutal experiment seemed to be going down in the mud and the blood of Cagliari, just as we were facing the truth, asking ourselves how in the name of God we were going to get anything out of this game with Packie hoofing the ball up the park to no-one in particular, the answer came — from Packie hoofing the ball up the park to no-one in particular.

In this case the recipient happened to be a member of his own team, Kevin Sheedy, who mis-controlled it towards Steve McMahon of England, just on the edge of his own area. It would be a goal as horrible in its creation as the England goal, since it was essentially made by a player on each side losing the ball, and all as a consequence of Packie's massive punt. Yet in execution it was beautiful.

In one instinctive and decisive movement, Sheedy had stolen it from McMahon and swept it with his educated left foot into the bottom right-hand corner of the net.

All of Ireland, and all Irish people all around the world, went mad with joy.

In Crosthwaite Park, we jumped around the room, roaring savagely.

At the RDS they would be seen erupting in drunken ecstasy, both in still photographs and in RTÉ pictures which captured this instant transformation from sombreness to crazy jubilation.

People who did not know one another hugged and kissed. Men told other men that they loved them.

Arthur appeared to be prostrate, in a quasi-Islamic posture, as if giving thanks to a personal God. At some point in the mêlée, my cigarette was extinguished and it was only when smoke was later seen billowing from the couch that we realised where the lit end had gone. Not that we cared about burning couches. Even if it was the one that Bono had sat on, telling old showband stories.

On the pitch, the reaction of Steve Staunton seemed especially demented, perhaps the Dundalk man in him responding with that extra bit of fervour to the blow which had been struck against the old enemy.

But there was still about 20 minutes to go. I can't recall any thought in our heads other than the thought of hanging on somehow. If the result stayed as it was, we would 'win'. It was not for us to be playing for an actual win at this stage, it was down to England to chase the victory which was the least expected of them by their unhappy followers and their demented newspapermen.

We were looking for a different sort of victory. One that would be celebrated with as much fervour as the Miracle of Stuttgart, though the dynamic was somewhat different. In Stuttgart we had been hanging on somehow for almost the entire match, whereas in Cagliari we had created a new narrative, one of redemption, of rescuing ourselves from the darkest fate imaginable. In Stuttgart the Fear that England might score had been total and undiluted until the final whistle; in Cagliari that particular Fear had gone early doors and we had moved into a new realm of dread from which we were rescued so fabulously by the Sheedy goal.

And now, of course, there was 20 minutes of a whole new form of dread to be endured. I recall dreading Gazza most of all, Gazza who seemed to be the only man in Sardinia on that night with any real interest in playing football and who was clearly capable of it too, which was especially worrying.

But we got away with it. And we felt that we were in good standing again with the baleful gods when the replay showed that Alan McLoughlin had been in an off-side position and that our goal might have been disallowed. Twelve years later, as he neared the end of his career with Forest Green Rovers, McLoughlin would tell Jon Henderson of *The Observer* that he knew he was offside: 'I quickly wheeled away to the right, and it was only after I'd run about ten yards, when I saw the linesman had kept his flag down, that I knew I'd got away with it.'

Fifty-thousand replays later, he was still clearly offside. But the goal would still stand.

How many times has the average Irish person seen the replay of that goal? From the kick-out by Bonner to the joust between Sheedy and MacMahon, to the ball flashing past Peter Shilton and then the players messily celebrating and the Green Army going berserk on the terraces it takes about 20 seconds. How many hours of our lives have we spent looking at that 20 seconds, indulging in what recovering alcoholics describe as 'euphoric recall?'

It is an apt description in the circumstances, as so many of us happened to be drunk at the time.

So we are euphorically recalling the goal and we are also recalling being drunk and the whole country apparently being drunk along with us.

Dion Fanning, remarkably, was sober on the night, presumably due to that slight complication of the Leaving starting the following morning. So he has a clear memory of getting into his car after the match with his brother Evan and driving from Dun Laoghaire into Dublin, blowing the horn.

He believes he was the first person in Dun Laoghaire, maybe the first person in Dublin to start blowing the horn, or at least he didn't hear anyone else blowing the horn until he started doing it himself. Maybe this was the horn we heard in Crosthwaite Park, one of many unfamiliar noises, the irresistible sound of people taking to the streets, the sound of *fiesta*.

Dion says the journey into town was unlike any we had known in this Republic, where men tended to blow their horns in delight only on their way to a wedding reception, fired up by the thrilling prospect of drinking for the rest of the day with a cast-iron excuse. With horns blaring and flags waving we might have been in some country where the people are unashamedly demonstrative, maybe somewhere in Latin America. But for the absence of indiscriminate gunfire, we might have been in Cameroon.

Such a night …

———

And there was the promise of more, with qualification from Group F now looking almost certain. Having come through this terrifying trial, we could only see good things happening in our next match against Egypt on Sunday. And we felt it reasonable to assume that Egypt would be beaten by Holland in their opening match the following night and then beaten by England in the third match, what with England needing the points after what we'd done to them tonight.

As we slumped in Crosthwaite Park, elated and utterly exhausted, euphoric recall was heaped upon euphoric recall, the images of this night already assuming the status of sacred icons.

One image above all was engraved on our consciousness and would become the next cover of *Hot Press*. It was the expression on Packie's face as he launched that huge kick in the general direction of Sheedy, the gritted teeth, a look of ferocious determination that we would not be beaten, that we would get ourselves out of this by sheer force of will.

Twice now, in major finals, we had come through this horrible ordeal and we were still standing, with Packie again the symbol of the resistance to England, either keeping them out in Stuttgart, or leading the charge in Sardinia.

If someone had come in at that moment and told us that this wasn't the right way to play football, that we were virtually bringing the game into disrepute with our brutalist style, we would have laughed. And we would have laughed scornfully at that critic who didn't seem to get it, who didn't understand that after all we'd been through, the result was the only thing that counted.

This is what success, or at least the absence of failure, was doing to us. And maybe this was our first glimpse of the spirit of the fat years that were to follow, this hard-headedness, this utter indifference about what you had to do, if you wanted to get ahead.

To hell with them all, we thought. We were claiming our little slice of happiness now, and not only were we not ashamed of the way we were playing, we revelled in it.

Chapter 12 ⌒

| THE SHAME

We revelled in it at least until Sunday.

I was still revelling in it the following day, when the intensity of the hangover took me out of the house on Sinnott Terrace and around the corner to the Cumberland Inn for the cure.

It is one of those surreal scenes which remains with me from that time of high surrealism, sitting in the Cumberland Inn in Dun Laoghaire at noon, drinking a pint of lager while the television showed a video of the match from the night before.

Drinking at noon, in the company of other happy drinkers and not feeling bad about it.

Drinking at noon and feeling that I was not alone, but taking part in some great national drink-a-thon, in which I was just playing my small-but-necessary part. And actually feeling better about everything, the morning after.

Later, I had to go to the Burlington Hotel to interview Philomena Begley for the *Sunday Independent*. So it was all getting a bit otherworldly. And stranger still, Jane and Roseanne and I were not just living in a house, we were living in a house with a phone in it. I have a distinct memory of ringing people up, just to tell them that I was talking to them on a phone that wasn't coin-operated.

And most bizarrely, the man who owned the house had been casually mentioning that he might be interested in selling it to us. For about £70,000, which seemed like an awful lot of money for a really small terraced house, even if it was in Dun Laoghaire. But we had gone to the local EBS anyway, just to talk about it, to see if it could be done. Apparently it could, though it was probably too big a step to contemplate when you're still getting used to the novelty of having a home-phone installed. But sitting there in the EBS manager's office, talking telephone numbers, was something we probably needed to do anyway, a rite of passage.

Again, I need to stress how deeply unnatural it felt to be even thinking of borrowing a large five-figure sum to buy a house, a procedure which, in a few years' time, would be regarded by most couples as a routine transaction, just to pay for the extension. In the fullness of time, a couple would be quite happy to borrow about half-a-million to buy a house just like the one in Sinnott Terrace, which we would eventually decide not to buy for 70 grand.

Not that such trivialities were uppermost in my mind, coming down after Cagliari and getting up again for Philomena Begley.

Credit was flowing all over the place, with the Credit Union now becoming a national joke in the best possible way, advancing a few quid here and a few quid there for vital life-saving operations, an extraordinarily high percentage of which would be taking place on the islands of Sicily and Sardinia, with follow-up procedures on the mainland of Italy itself. It was estimated at one stage that an evacuation of 30,000 people was taking place, that the Paddies were arriving in Italy from all over the world, many of them seeking specialist treatments which were only to be had in the finest facilities in Cagliari and Palermo, in Genoa and Rome.

Haughey would eventually be arriving on the government jet, apparently not minding any more that we were all living above our means. Not that he had minded much in the first place. But perhaps for the first time there was a sense that it wasn't just people like Haughey who could enjoy themselves on someone else's dime, that Paddy the postman and Paddy the bus conductor and Paddy who didn't actually work at all, could open a line of credit just to go off on the tear. And not feel bad about it.

Because there was a growing understanding of something that the rich had always known, that enjoying yourself is not necessarily a waste of time and money. That having a laugh is good for the soul, and that if enough people are doing it at the same time, it is good for the country. And if you need a mortgage to play your part, so be it.

No more would it be considered sinful to be borrowing money for reasons that would once have been regarded as unorthodox, or even downright peculiar. We were starting to realise there was such a thing as an 'intangible benefit', that a dose of money could give a boost to your morale or to your sense of belonging that even poor Paddy was entitled to, enjoying the sheer fun of having a few quid in his pocket and of going off to Italy — yes, we were showering ourselves with intangible benefits, albeit at the relatively modest levels permitted at the time by the most prudent financial institutions.

Paddy had always had a profligate streak, but unlike the rich, he could not rightly indulge it without also being visited by feelings of guilt and shame. So this wasn't just about the willingness to get ourselves into a bit of debt, for something that might be regarded as frivolous. It was perhaps the moment when Paddy felt good enough about himself to declare that he would decide what was frivolous, and what was not. He, and not the Bank of Ireland or even the good old Credit Union, would make that judgment call. Maybe we were learning how to live a bit.

Now we just had to learn how to afford it.

———

But first I had to interview Philomena Begley, an oddly poignant occasion in the circumstances. Philomena was one of those legends of Irish entertainment who had become about as successful as you can be, in Ireland. She was a first-rate country singer who had recorded some really classy duets with Ray Lynam, in the style of George Jones and Tammy Wynette. And yet even the most accomplished of those showband musicians would somehow never have the confidence to write their own material, to assert themselves as artists the way that the rockers would. They did not dare to ask for too much, perhaps out of fear that it would all be taken away from them, for their impertinence. Why would they need to be making it in Britain or in America, in the places that mattered, when they had a fine house in the midlands with ornamental guitars on the gate and enough time on their hands to be playing golf four times a week?

So on such a day, when everything seemed possible for the Republic of Ireland, it was like remembering old times to be talking to one of those who had always settled for less. And I had the advantage of viewing her through this shimmering haze of alcohol in which I, and most of my countrymen and many of my country-women, too, were becoming enveloped.

It was an advantage, at least, as long as we were winning, or not getting beaten by England. But it was about to get a tad more complicated, because Egypt would unexpectedly draw 1-1 with Holland.

And it would get more complicated still, in Palermo.

———

How bad were we, in Palermo, against Egypt? It is hard to quantify, because we weren't doing much that was essentially different to what we usually did. We got a scoreless draw, which would normally do us, but we needed something a bit more than that to calm the nerves.

It was now becoming clear that Jack's methods worked best when the other team was trying to play football and we were trying to stop them — because usually we would succeed. And ideally we would both get the result that we needed and we would move on.

We would succeed because the system was all about the avoidance of risk, but also because most of the players were pretty good, and some of them were exceptional. In fact, George Byrne and I would get through a fair few slow evenings in the International comparing the Republic first eleven to the England first eleven, and invariably arriving at the conclusion that the Republic was better, not just as a unit, but man for man — the same could not be said of any Irish team before or since. Even Andy Townsend, who was preferred by Jack though he was clearly not in the same class as, say, Ronnie Whelan, would have been coveted by the England team of that time.

So by convincing these good players to do all the things he wanted them to do when they didn't have the ball, Jack's team became damnably hard to beat. But when they did have the ball, as they did against Egypt, it seemed that they had forgotten what to do with it.

Not that Jack was a vociferous opponent of good football — he was cuter than that in getting his way. For example, when the lads went a bit mad on that night in Hanover and started playing football against the Russians, Jack didn't intervene and call a halt to it. He let it happen, because it was clearly working for him. But the players also knew that the moment it went wrong, Jack would be on their case.

It tends to work like this — players will want to play if they are encouraged to play, if they feel that they're allowed to make a mistake and still carry on playing creatively and constructively, but if they are not encouraged, if they know they will get hammered as soon as anything goes wrong, eventually they will just do what the boss tells them to do. By now, any of that footballing spirit had been drained out of the Republic, so that even a sudden eruption in the style of Hanover was no longer feasible. They had every other type of spirit, but not the type that creates a goal for you against an obdurate opponent such as Egypt.

So how bad were we?

Well, for the purposes of this book I did something that very few Irish people have ever done before — I actually looked again at Ireland's matches in Italia 90, all the way through.

And I did it completely sober.

Dion Fanning happened to have the videos stashed away as souvenirs of the time, rather than for football reasons. For we know that this story is not really about football, as such, but there was a certain element of football involved in it, and it's all still on tape.

And it is bad, bad, bad stuff.

So much of it reminds you of that old line about two bad teams having an off-day. Even the best bits, such as the goal against England or the other one we would score against Holland, seem to exemplify the barbarity of it all, the shameless punting of the ball up the park, in the hope of getting a lucky break and forcing it into the net somehow and then running round like men possessed, 'Until our legs were worn down to stumps,' as John Aldridge put it, killing the game.

Football had been going through a bad time for several years leading up to Italia 90, and not just because of the 'ooligans. The European Cup Final of 1986 is remembered as an abomination, a rock-bottom moment when men realised that the game was in very deep trouble, with Barcelona trying to play a bit of football against Steaua Bucharest and eventually giving up, the both of them settling for extra time and penalties which, with a sinister inevitability, were won by Steaua.

Later we learned that the team was the plaything of Nicu Ceauşescu, son of the dictator, and that the goalkeeper, Duckadam, who saved the penalties, had been given a present of a Porsche by a rich guy who was a fanatical supporter of Real Madrid, so delighted was he that they had beaten Madrid's mortal enemies, Barcelona. According to legend, when they got back behind the Iron Curtain, Nicu demanded that Duckadam give him the car, and when the goalkeeper declined, his fingers were broken by Nicu's enforcers.

It is a legend that I don't want to believe, and yet in the times that were in it, you could easily believe such things.

It wasn't just that teams were playing cynically for penalties because they weren't capable of playing any other way, it seemed that they were playing this anti-football even when they were well able to play the game properly.

There was always a touch of blackguardism in teams from the old Eastern bloc, and it had stopped them winning anything of con-sequence — though they were always producing footballers with superb technique, they somehow preferred to do it the cynical way, the wrong way.

Now at last it seemed to be working for them, with Steaua's graceless victory. And it was in this global context that the game itself was being scrutinised in a fundamental way, to see if it could be made more difficult for the cynics, if it could be reformed.

At this dark time for the game, here came the Republic achieving ominous levels of success with the goalkeeper as playmaker, playing this strange and horrible football, which to the aficionados looked as cynical as anything out of Ceaușescu's Romania — without the little flashes of class.

We were doing it the wrong way — except to us, the best fans in the world, there was no wrong way to do this extraordinary thing that we were doing. Perhaps only Irish people truly understood where it was coming from, this hybrid of Gaelic football and Association football, this first truly successful Compromise Rules format. For years the GAA and the Australian Rules organisations had been trying to combine aspects of their two codes, creating a new game which seemed only to bring out the worst in all concerned, resulting in scenes of grotesque violence and chaos on an unprecedented scale.

Now Jack had stumbled onto this new code, in which you didn't have to change the shape of the ball, but like the Aussies trying to get accustomed to the round ball, the 'soccer' players would have to set aside a lot of what came naturally to them, in order to avail of the best of the Gaelic code — most notably, the incessant chasing and harrying, and the high, lobbing, dropping balls sent up the field by Packie. Helpfully, Packie had played a lot of Gaelic football in his youth And so had Niall Quinn, who would often be there at the other end to 'pull' on Packie's dropping balls.

Maybe we helped to change the game of football for good, because this would be the last World Cup before the introduction of three points for a win to discourage draws, and the new back-pass rule, which meant that the keeper would have far fewer opportunities to settle himself and take his time before launching it into the firmament.

Looking back, FIFA never did bend the rules to have us play in Boston or Chicago or Rome, but maybe they changed the rules for all time, with us at least partly in mind.

Maybe we drove them to it.

——

If there was one game in which attitudes hardened irretrievably, it was in Palermo when we got together with Egypt to produce one of the worst games of professional football ever seen.

It is perhaps a mark of my inexplicable complacency that I had opted to watch this one on the big screen upstairs in the Purty Kitchen, that Liam and Arthur and I hadn't precisely replicated our arrangements of the previous Monday, up to and including the cold cuts and the cherry tomatoes and maybe even the couch going on fire.

I can only say in my defence that there seemed to be good ju-ju in the Purty Loft for me, as it was there I had watched us slaughtering Norn Iron 3-0 in the qualifying group — or at least slaughtering them in the second half.

And all around the country, all around the world indeed, wherever green is worn, they were gathering at such venues, the most celebrated of which was the Submarine Bar in Crumlin. So successful had the proprietors been in creating an Italia-90 atmosphere, that street traders had set up stalls outside the pub, selling hats and flags and favours. Extra security staff had to be hired to stop people climbing through the windows of the Conservatory Lounge. A full-sized goal was erected on the flat roof with flashing green, white and gold lights and a dummy goalkeeper who at one point was reported stolen — he had been smuggled into the ladies' toilet, causing some drunken consternation.

It seemed that you'd be missing some vital part of the experience, if you didn't watch at least one of the matches on a big screen somewhere, if you didn't move beyond your circle of friends to embrace the wider community — we were all friends now. Though I have never much liked the big-screen deal, not just because of the foul memories of Palermo, but because the pubs are full of people who know nothing about football and who keep reacting in the wrong way to the wrong things: they will start roaring with anticipation, seeing a shot that can't possibly result in the goal that they are preparing to hail and most damningly, they have even been known to cheer wildly to celebrate a goal that they think has been scored — even when it's just about to hit the bar and rebound to safety.

I am maddened by these people because they disturb my ancient rhythms, which are already disturbed enough by the tension and by the effects of alcohol. And you would hear things like this: the Egyptians won't be able to cope with the long ball from Packie because they come from a sandy country, where the ball doesn't bounce the same way — this was a popular pre-match analysis in the Purty Loft in the feverish moments before kick-off.

The weather was beautiful in Dublin that day. There were flags and bunting and even kerbstones being painted green, white and orange — were we seeing a touch of Englishness here? It is said that in one Dublin church, the priest and the altar boys were dressed in green and white garments and as the Mass came to an end the priest addressed the people: 'My friends, I'm sure that the hearts of every person in Ireland will be with our team and supporters this afternoon. Let me finish off this Mass by asking you to join in a special hymn.' The priest then took a tricolour from underneath the pulpit, began waving it and singing and the whole congregation joined in: 'Olé! Olé! Olé!'

In his pre-match analysis, Eamon Dunphy had this vision: 'This is for the whole country,' he said, 'And the team is a catalyst. The character of our people out there, the team … they haven't had one yellow card. And the way we've celebrated the whole thing is glorious and golden and it's for every single person, all the kids, all the players, everybody's involved and everybody's made a contribution.'

But it was the post-match analysis that would hit the spot.

'Anyone who sends a team out to play like that should be ashamed of themselves', he said. 'We know about the upside of Jack. We know how hard these lads work. We know about their courage. But football is a two-sided game, when you haven't got the ball and when you have got the ball. When we got the ball we were cowardly, ducking out of taking responsibility.

'I feel embarrassed for soccer, embarrassed for the country, embarrassed for all the good players, for our great tradition in soccer. This is nothing to do with the players who played today. That's a good side. I feel embarrassed and ashamed of that performance, and we should be.' And he threw his pen down, as if throwing down the gauntlet.

It was a challenge which would not be refused in the days to come, but in the Purty Loft, most of us were too depressed to be analysing Dunphy's analysis. In fact everything he said, before and after, seemed accurately to reflect the feelings of the multitudes —

we had plunged from a manic high to a manic low and a lot of us now had a lot of drink taken.

Ireland, at this moment, was in a bad place.

Chapter 13 ~

AGAINST THE RUN OF PLAY

Eamon Dunphy lives in the moment. In a human being this can be disastrous, in a TV analyst it is a priceless gift. And it is a gift which belongs more in the grand tradition of showbusiness than that of journalism, in the conventional sense.

The journalist of the old school will usually have a checking mechanism, reminding him that he is being inconsistent. He can't plunge from euphoria to revulsion in the style of Dunphy before and after Egypt, without feeling some need to explain, to declare in some mealy-mouthed fashion that he may appear to be contradicting himself, but he has been left with no option, due to this unfortunate and unexpected turn of events.

Dunphy doesn't bother with that shit. Living in the moment, he calls it as he is feeling it in the moment. Which can sometimes lead to him apparently contradicting himself, in the course of a three-hour football special — indeed, it is not unknown for him to be feeling different about something at the end of a sentence than he felt when he was starting out.

But then most of us who are watching TV are living in the moment, too, and we have busy lives, so when he moves on, we move on with him.

In those days Dunphy was also writing a column for the *Sunday Independent*, work which was compared by the journalist Sam Smyth to that of an opera singer — the articles were like arias, grand statements of high emotion, where the practitioner is front and centre and bursting with adrenaline, not sitting down in the dark in the front row scribbling into a notebook with the other critics, broken down by the tyranny of fact.

And while he had made his name in newspapers, originally with the *Sunday Tribune*, writing about football and about the wretchedness of the League of Ireland in particular, it was during this time with the *Sunday Independent* that Dunphy really found his voice. Instead of just writing about the serious business of football, he could be found offering his opinions on the more light-hearted and trashy aspects of Irish society such as politics and public service broadcasting.

Which in retrospect seems like a natural development, though at the time it took the *Sunday Indo* Editor Aengus Fanning to figure that one out. To decide that there was no law against football men writing about other aspects of the human condition, if they were able to do it.

There is also a complicated theory that the *Sunday Indo* became a great success at this time, not because it was championing the pluralist attitudes which were becoming general all over Ireland, or because it was implacably opposed to the IRA, or because gossip columnist Terry Keane was known to be having an affair with Charlie Haughey, or because the likes of Dunphy and Sam Smyth and Veronica Guerin and Colm Tóibín and Anthony Cronin were writing for it, but essentially because I had started to write for it.

It is a theory that you don't hear too often, though it has at least one strong advocate — my mother.

And as for myself, I have always found working for the *Sunday Indo* about as uncomplicated as anything can be in this life.

There was a message for me one day in the *Hot Press*, that Aengus Fanning had called. I had heard of Aengus Fanning, but I wasn't sure what he did exactly. A passing Jackie Hayden, General Manager of *Hot Press*, told me he was Editor of the *Sunday Independent*.

Aengus got back to me later, wondering if I'd be interested in working for the paper. I told him I would.

A few weeks later I answered the phone in the hall and it was Anne Harris, asking me to write an article about Hal Roach, which I assumed was to be written in whatever way I had been writing other articles for *Hot Press* or the *Irish Press* or whomever, because I couldn't do it any other way.

So I did that — Dermot Morgan performed the highlights of Hal's repertoire for me over the phone, in Hal's voice — and I brought it in, and they then paid me more than anyone else had ever done. They were also exceptionally nice to me and they asked me straight away if there was anything else I wanted to do — still not very complicated, but it seemed to be working.

And yet there is this nostalgia now among media folk for the hungry years of *Hot Press* and *Magill* and *In Dublin*, many of whose contributors are now well known. We wonder how it all sort-of faded away when Ireland hit the big-time, how the fine young energies of the next generation got diverted into other things, where you might have the vague prospect of eventually making something approaching the average industrial wage. Because you wouldn't start writing for these publications for the money: you were getting your big break and you were getting your opportunity to bring the government down on a monthly basis and you were getting free drink and free cocktail sausages and free triangular sandwiches, but you wouldn't be getting rich any time soon.

And because we weren't living in a money economy, as such, many of us never fully adjusted to the notion of actually getting paid a living wage for this thing we do. Most of us who started out in magazines at that time had no idea about what we could or should get paid.

John Waters recalls 'haggling' with Vincent Browne over a fee for a column about RTÉ daytime radio which he had been asked to do for the *Sunday Tribune*. Browne was adamant that he didn't want any of Waters' opinions in this column, none whatsoever, not even the vaguest suggestion of a point of view, he just wanted to be told what had been on the radio. Waters clearly couldn't get his head around something so stultifying and he knew there would be a confrontation about something else, too, the difficult subject of money.

For days, he had steeled himself for the meeting. It had been suggested to him that you could actually make a bit of money at this journalism and John was determined not to sell himself short.

'How much do you want to get paid for that?' Browne said.

John summoned up all his courage. 'I want fifty pounds a week', he said.

Browne was horrified. 'You can't fucking work for fifty pounds a week,' he said. 'I'll give you eighty to start and we'll review it in a few weeks.'

Just like that, he had beaten him down.

We had no proper concept of money because we were still in a better place than we ever imagined we would be; we could never get it out of our heads that if we weren't going over to London to interview Robbie Robertson, we would be playing a game of darts in some pub in the midlands, and we would be doing that, and nothing but that, for the rest of our lives. We still couldn't quite figure out how this thing had happened to us.

'It was all against the run of play', Waters told me once. He reminded me that he was making his daily deliveries in a Hiace van in Castlerea when Niall Stokes phoned him to enquire, not if he might fancy doing another review of Horslips somewhere out in the west, but if by any chance he might be available to fly out immediately to do a piece on Dire Straits in Paris.

'We were innocent enough to be amazed by such things, but we never imagined that if our lives kept getting magically better in this way, we would acquire any power in the conventional sense, of being allowed to participate in the running of an institution', Waters recalls. 'Nothing belonged to us except the air, into which we could proclaim the things we loved and the things we hated — this is a great album, this is a shite album. The only power we had, is that we could say whatever we liked. And we felt we had the right to say whatever we liked, because we cared about these things, because they were important and because they had changed our lives.'

And evidently we regarded this as such a precious thing in itself, we thought that about fifty quid a week would cover the rest.

So when I was paid a three-figure sum for my first contribution to the *Sunday Independent*, I was shocked. Of course I was deliriously happy, and yet I also had this feeling of guilt — for all our rock 'n' roll attitude, the young journalists of the 1980s could not get away from these ancient weaknesses, which had held Paddy back for so long.

I particularly recall that day on the third floor of the old *Indo* building on Middle Abbey Street, when I brought in the Hal Roach piece and Aengus went off to make us coffee, as Anne sat there trying to read my typed sheets about Hal, with the amendments written in biro — I had always assumed that the editors of national newspapers were the sort of men who would order coffee to be brought to them. I can only conclude that Aengus was making the coffee for us that day, because it was less complicated than getting someone else to do it.

————

The least complicated thing to do with Dunphy — and thus by far the best thing — was just to let him fire away. It was probably the polar opposite to the Charlton style of management, which would never have tolerated a soloist like Dunphy, let alone encouraged him and given him the reassurance that if he screwed it up, he would be supported — massive libel damages of three hundred grand to Proinsias de Rossa would back that up, baby!

But if the *Sunday Indo* had put him on the main stage, Dunphy's post-match comments were about to put him where a man of his enthusiasms ultimately needs to be — front and centre. It was exhilarating, but it was also a very dangerous place for him, because Dunphy had stirred the mob instinct that is always latent in such a gathering of the multitudes.

There was an ornery mood across the land, in the aftermath of that horrible match in Palermo, and there was a need to direct that bad feeling towards something or somebody. We couldn't really bring ourselves to direct it towards Jack and the lads, because this was not a search for the truth here, it was a need to rid ourselves of a world of bile.

So, in a text-book example of how the mob is aroused, Dunphy's comments started to get twisted ever so slightly, and soon it was widely accepted as fact that he had declared that he was ashamed to be Irish.

At some level, the mob must have known that this was not what he'd said at all. But they weren't being reasonable at this moment, they weren't interested in nuances, they were looking for something to hate.

And anyway, what is wrong with being ashamed to be Irish, now and again? There is no country in the world which doesn't have a few things to be ashamed about, and we, who had harboured the IRA and the Magdalene Laundries, can throw our hat into the ring with any of them.

But that is a rational assessment, and we were not in a rational frame of mind: we were seething, because this had been a supremely happy time, until now. These were the best days of our lives, and just when we had started to get carried away by the good of it all, we were hauled back and told we were no good and we'd be going home soon, probably in disgrace.

Not surprisingly, the first man to inform us of this was going to be a tad unpopular — especially if he was the same man who had been extolling the beauty of the moment at the start of the show.

In this great gathering, much had been made of the fact that our Italia 90 had spread way beyond football, bringing in the entire population of the country, which included a load of people who knew nothing about football.

Now, at this extremely tricky stage, we realised that not knowing about football could be something of a drawback, that too few of the folks knew enough about football, to know that football deals in the truth, that you can't get away from the realities of scoring and letting in goals or not scoring at all, that the bottom line can't be finessed and the result can't be made to look any better by a PR company.

Giles and Dunphy had been educating us about the superior nature of football values for some time, but still we were finding it hard to take.

Football is not business or finance and it is not politics, where all that bullshit works, all the time. Which may help to explain why it seems so alien to so many of the panellists on *Questions and Answers*, who have thrived in that world of bullshit, and who simply can't make the step up in class, to treat of more substantial matters.

But the fact that Dunphy was right about the performance against Egypt did not in any way placate the baying hordes. He could even be accused of being too lenient on Jack, of going on the attack only when the result went the wrong way, but in fairness to him, he had written about the ugly side. He had argued in the *Sunday Indo* that David O'Leary had been treated appallingly by Jack, who preferred the clearly inferior Mick McCarthy, for his own ideological reasons.

And there were times when Jack himself couldn't hide the ugliness, most notably in comments quoted in Paul Rowan's

The Team That Jack Built, in which Jack describes why he picked an unusual team featuring Stapleton, Brady and Tony Galvin for a pre-World Cup warm-up game against Germany: 'With Ireland, you see, they don't give up their fuckin' heroes easily, so you've really got to show 'em. If I don't pick Liam to play or I don't pick Kevin Moran to play or I don't pick somebody who's Irish and who's been there a long time, they want to know why you don't fuckin' pick him to play. And you say, "Well, he's too old, he's not fast enough now. I want somebody who can do better for us in the years to come, and I've got to re-shape the side." So what I did was, I put 'em on display. I had three of them — Liam, Frank and Tony Galvin — who were coming to the end of their time and I put 'em on display to the public.'

Stapleton ruined the display by scoring and generally playing very well, leaving Jack with virtually no option but to include him in the panel for Italia 90, a move which Jack would bitterly regret, telling Rowan that Stapleton had been a moaner and a pain in the arse to him.

But it was Brady's last match for Ireland. Jack substituted him after half an hour and put on Townsend instead, a move which so infuriated Brady he resigned from international football, insisting that he had been humiliated by Jack, that he should at least have been substituted at half-time.

Ugly, ugly stuff, this 'putting 'em on display'.

Still, we should probably be more forgiving about the things men say when they're riled. I have learned that in people of talent, there is often a blind spot, or three or four blind spots — and that goes for Dunphy as well as for Jack.

So now that the ugly stuff wasn't even working any more, we couldn't find it in our hearts to turn on Jack, after all he had done for us. So we turned on Dunphy instead. When you're living in a beautiful bubble, you just don't want to know about that ugly stuff.

Italia 90 may have given us a foretaste of the Tiger, but not necessarily in the way that the corporate dudes claim, with their talk of 'confidence'. Maybe the boom was most like the Charlton years in the sense that it was a bubble, maybe with less spontaneity than the original, but created by our desperate desire to be free of all that held us back, sustained by a degree of self-deception, a lot of talk about what a great people we are, a certain amount of borrowing and a lot of drinking. And while it worked for us for a long time, it also meant that we had to give up certain things that were part of our better nature, the way that we gave up Liam Brady and had very little use for Ronnie Whelan or David O'Leary.

It's not that Paddy suddenly got good at everything some time in the mid-1990s, no more than we suddenly got good at football in 1987. If you recall, in the first pages of this book Paddy was on Broadway and at Carnegie Hall and selling shedloads of U2 albums, so we had always had a flair for what you might call the finer things of life. And you don't end up on Broadway without 'confidence', you don't end up at Carnegie Hall without knowing how to make a few quid either.

But perhaps the Charlton years showed us how to make the ugly stuff work for us as well. How to make money out of boybands and chick-lit and Irish dancing, the way we made our mark on the World Cup, doing it Jack's way.

And not being ashamed of it.

Except perhaps, for a little while, one afternoon in Palermo.

Chapter 14 ∿

∣ SAME AGAIN PLEASE

Dunphy's car was surrounded at the airport and it was rocked from side to side by a bunch of blackguards, with Dunphy inside it.

It was a very, very ugly scene.

But when they look back on it, even these renegades of the Green Army would have to concede that Dunphy was bringing something to the party, because a great story needs a few dark interludes, a few moments when disaster seems inevitable but is somehow averted. And we had had several of these during the England match alone, quite apart from this protracted agony-in-the-garden in the days before the last match of the Group, against Holland.

The climactic nature of this encounter had cranked everything up to a new level of madness. It was anticipated that the entire population of the country would be watching it, that you'd be able to walk down O'Connell Street on Thursday evening without meeting a soul, apart perhaps from the photographer who would be taking this unique picture of the main thoroughfare of a capital city, deserted — but who would take that photograph?

It wasn't good enough any more to assume that a woman photographer would take it, because the women had also succumbed. Since so many of the 'social' struggles of the 1980s concerned them and what they were or were not entitled to do with their lives, it seems that women, too, were seeing Italia 90 as the perfect opportunity to wind down and to let themselves go. And as Nell

McCafferty would point out, the women were indirectly paying for a lot of it, because the men were spending money in places like Sicily, or maybe just down at the Submarine Bar, that would otherwise be frittered away on household items such as food and clothing for the children.

But perhaps the most unheralded contribution of the women at this time was the way they facilitated the drinking.

Rightly or wrongly, Paddy has always felt that women are a controlling presence in this area, a barrier to his full enjoyment of the drinking life. He sees them essentially in a policing role. When he is watching football on television, for example, sipping a few cans of cool beer, and slipping into a state of deep, deep relaxation, the voice of woman seems to call him back from that happy place. And no matter what she is saying, this is all he can hear: 'Stop relaxing … stop relaxing … stop relaxing …'

Paddy has always found it hard to relax. There is no stillness in him, no quietude in his restless soul. So the month-long festival of football and drinking that was Italia 90, seemed to offer to him the prospect of the deepest relaxation he would ever have, a spiritual journey.

Of course, there would be moments of terrible tension and anxiety too, but even they would be experienced in the context of this broader peace that he was enjoying, this retreat from the world, into the World Cup.

And yet he could not share this inner vision with his life's partner. He could share it only with other men, who had an effortless understanding of it.

So when women started to catch the Italia-90 virus in large numbers, there was an historical moment of reconciliation between two equal and opposite forces — and there was no need for women to know the off-side rule or to know anything about anything. All that was needed was their indulgence.

The Berlin Wall had come down in 1989, and in Ireland a fair few monuments to repression had been coming down, too. But the collapse of this particular Wall, between the drinking football man and the women of Ireland, was a marvellous thing to behold. Some critical mass of irresponsibility had been reached, which allowed women to desert their posts and to join the party.

In the build-up to one of the matches, on Philipsburgh Avenue, the poet and broadcaster Theo Dorgan remembers seeing a group of elderly Dublin women, attired in the national colours, lined up on a street in a state of high excitement, doing the can-can.

Women realised at some point that all the normal laws of nature had been suspended, so they might as well go with it. They might as well get themselves a funny hat and a big inflatable hammer in the Ireland colours and go down to the pub and stand there shouting at the big screen like everyone else — it was too late to stop now. Maybe it was something about the men so openly displaying their emotions, men crying in public, that attracted them. Maybe they, too, just felt like getting drunk after all they'd been through, and decided that here was the perfect excuse.

And it was a wise call, in that respect, because we have a perspective on this, which confirms that Italia 90 was indeed the greatest excuse ever to go drinking in the history of Ireland.

We have the perspective of the Tiger years, during which Paddy developed a near-genius for thinking up new excuses to go drinking, from the regular corporate lunch to the stag-weekend in Vilnius, to the pheasant shooting and the feasting that would follow, but nothing compares and nothing will ever compare to Italia 90 as the ultimate cast-iron guilt-free all-singing all-dancing excuse to go drinking.

Men knew this, and women knew this and children knew this. Indeed, men and women would have children as a result of this, with a World Cup baby boom materialising in 1991. But there would be a rough side to it, too, represented in Sebastian Barry's play, *The Pride of Parnell Street*, which has at its core an episode of wife-beating during Italia 90. And during the madness, I remember witnessing a delightful scene one day in the People's Park in Dun Laoghaire, whereby three generations of a family, a grandmother, a young couple and two small children, were partaking of some sort of a picnic. The grandmother was holding what can only be described as a large bottle of whiskey.

A charming tableau.

But it is impossible to look at any set of photographs of Irish people at that time, without seeing extraordinary quantities of drink and extraordinary levels of drunkenness. There are men lying on the floor face down, lost to the world. There are men sitting on toilet seats with their trousers pulled down, smiling at the camera, wearing a Viking helmet. There are men lying on a pavement on some foreign boulevard, comatose after the night before, almost naked, an empty bottle of cider and a few cans of beer still standing beside them. There are men lying on unmade beds in some foreign boarding house, sleeping during the day, with maybe a chair or a picture or even a television on the bed beside them, put there by their friends as a joke.

There are men vomiting. There are men on their knees vomiting into the toilet bowl, or just vomiting anywhere they feel like it. There are men vomiting because they are extremely ill from alcoholic poisoning and men vomiting almost as a form of self-expression.

Everywhere, there are men pissing, and laughing at the fact that they are pissing. There are men pissing into ashtrays. There are men with condoms filled with vodka, laughing hysterically at the camera as they drink the vodka. There are men drinking bottles of beer and bottles of spirits as they pose for a group photograph, fifteen of them on the bonnet of a car. There are men wearing vests and shorts leaving flowers with the porter at the front door of the maternity hospital, where their wives and newborns are resting, indicating that they are too drunk to go in there themselves.

Somehow Paddy, in these scenes of utter abandon, can't help drawing attention to the depths of the repression he must be feeling in the normal run of events.

Who amongst us can exclude ourselves from this part of the story? Because it was more than just the greatest excuse to go drinking; it was an excuse to go drinking in ways that we had never gone drinking before.

Other than tee-totallers, there is hardly a man alive in Ireland today who does not have some blissful memory of being terribly, terribly drunk during Italia 90 in the middle of the day, or some strange hour at which he had never been drunk before.

It was suitably Mediterranean, except your Mediterraneans wouldn't be throwing fourteen pints of stout into them as they lunched *al fresco*. We just couldn't do it any other way. We are anxious enough to begin with and that is partly why we drink, so the arrival of this great flood of anxiety was always going to carry us way over the limit. Not that that is the only reason why we drink, which helps to explain how I had written most of the first chapter of this book before realising that virtually every man I had mentioned thus far was an alcoholic or a recovering alcoholic — and they were the guys who were doing pretty well for themselves.

Norman Mailer had a theory about why the Irish drink so much. It came out in a story told by Frank McCourt to the *Sunday Independent*'s Barry Egan about his friend Joe Flaherty, who had run Mailer's campaign for mayor of New York during the 1970s. Joe had testicular cancer and was in hospital. Frank went to see him and noted that he looked especially tired that day.

'Jesus, yeah, Norman was just here,' said Joe. 'He had another one of his theories.'

Mailer's theory was that the Irish drink so much because they have an over-supply of semen and hormones and if they didn't drink, they would go raving mad. It's only a theory, but personally I wouldn't rule it out. You couldn't rule anything out, when you're dealing with something on this scale.

My own theory, or one of them, is that alcoholism is a form of immaturity. And that immaturity is an acute problem among the Irish, particularly the Irish male. We tend either to be late developers, or not to develop at all. From the day a man starts drinking too much, to the day he stops, it is arguable that he stays the same age, emotionally and psychologically. He is just not able to grow up properly, because he reacts to most difficult situations by drinking, thus avoiding whatever lessons might be learned.

There has been much useful work done on the reasons for the repeated failures of the Irish State and the various collapses of the Irish economy by journalists such as Kevin Myers, but my own intuition tells me to look at the immaturity of Paddy, because alcoholism is a form of immaturity, and we keep screwing everything up in a way that deeply resembles the behaviour patterns of the alcoholic.

We can have periods of prosperity, when we are 'on the dry', as it were, but because we don't address the fundamental issues, we keep relapsing into the old ways. We always secretly reserve the right to 'hang one on', to throw away what we have gained and to return to the darkness.

Even those of us who are not alcoholics, are not exactly grownups either.

And when you throw in all those who *are* alcoholics, and who are in positions of influence, you start to get a sense of where we might be going wrong.

It has been observed that the way we collectively behaved during the boom years was a bit like Paddy winning a massive compo claim and spending the money exuberantly until it all runs out, at which point he expresses great surprise that such a strange thing should have happened, just when everything was going so well.

Kevin Myers has mused much on our astonishing inability or refusal to plan things properly, or to plan them at all. Thus we can build hundreds of miles of motorways with no service areas, and we think that's all right. We have this delinquent streak, tending repeatedly towards self-destruction.

We seem to be uncomfortable with any strategy other than making it up as we go along, which may explain how so many of the Irish got around Italy in 1990, improvising, living on their wits, scraping together the means of survival and looking after the drunk ones, knowing that in a very short time, they would have to be looking after you. I guess you could keep that going, all right, for about three weeks.

And we viewed it as normal that men would spend nine-tenths of their money on gargle on the first night on foreign soil, caring nothing for the morrow.

We don't seem to have any idea what to do with money apart from to waste it. And we have a genius for that. All of which are the classic traits of the teenager on the beer, the immature person.

Or maybe I just favour this theory, because it seems to describe my own condition. In many ways I allowed my teenage years to continue all the way through my twenties and into my thirties. I had taken on vast responsibilities, quite casually, without realising that I might have to become a fully functioning adult, too, in order to make it all work. And in my case, that would mean making an agonising reappraisal of my drinking.

Which would mean basically giving it up.

But all this is much clearer now in hindsight.

One of the reasons we don't rightly grasp these things at the time is because the drink itself is stopping us from getting there — it is, as they say, cunning, baffling, powerful. We are still getting something out of it, still getting the message that everything is going to work out fine and that *we* are all right, it is everyone else who is wrong.

As far as I could discern, I was mainly a social drinker, doing a job which demanded that I socialise, and drink. At the time of Italia 90 I was drinking no more than many people I knew, though I now realise that many people I knew were either alcoholics themselves or getting there.

I was working all the time and apparently doing well and I could hardly stay sober for that long if I had some deep-seated problem, could I? It would take me a long time to understand that I was working mainly in order to create a space to drink, that that first pint in Mulligan's after I dropped in my copy had become a holy thing, if not the entire point of the exercise.

It is so hard to tell the points at which you are crossing into more dangerous territory, all you know is that when you find yourself there, you can't get back. Well, there is one way of getting back, but that means not drinking again, and that can seem pretty unimaginable.

I can't tell for sure if I crossed into those badlands during Italia 90, I just know that by the end of the year Jane and I weren't living together any more.

And it most certainly didn't feel like it back then, but maybe it was better that way. I was about 19 years old at the time, regardless of what it said on my birth certificate.

I would still see a lot of Roseanne, because I was only around the corner, in Monkstown. I would have to start growing up somehow, although I didn't start to understand that for about another five years.

First, I would need to improve my typing skills.

And I hope this is entirely coincidental, but it was only in writing this book that I realised that I stopped drinking for good at Christmas 1995 — which was just a few weeks after Jack resigned, having failed to qualify for Euro 96. At the time I didn't see a direct connection. Or even an indirect connection. I don't remember thinking that the Charlton years were now at an end, the good times were over, that it was time we all cleaned up our act, but I'm inclined to wonder if I was subconsciously responding to these deeper rhythms.

It just seems like too much of coincidence, that I finally came of age at the end of this roistering saga of football and beer, this bubble in which we would stay forever young. Thankfully, that other bubble would be along soon, the money-bubble, in which we could divert ourselves. But it is tempting to see the Charlton years as the last big blow-out for Paddy in general, his wild years before the onset of maturity, or at least the trappings of maturity.

Jack leaving us in 1995, his work here done, was supposed to signal the end of Paddy's growing pains — or maybe it was just the beginning of the end.

Or maybe we weren't even ready for that yet.

All of which was a long way from our minds as we waited, in a state of high anxiety, to see what Ruud Gullit and Frank Rijkaard and Marco Van Basten would do to us below in Palermo.

Chapter 15

OUTSIDE, IT'S LATIN AMERICA

We were taking no chances this time.

Arthur and I would be watching this in Liam's place, sitting on exactly the same couches, arranged in exactly the same way as they had been against England. We wouldn't be needing the cold cuts this time, or the cherry tomatoes, we were only fooling ourselves that food had any part to play in this episode. This would be a hard-drinking deal, from start to finish, though I should add that Arthur had a much healthier relationship with alcohol than I did, and it is a testament to the state we were in that he wanted it so much at this time.

Dunphy had gone out to Italy, which was probably the safest place for him. His trip had been planned long before the pen-throwing outrage, but most of us preferred to think of it as a showdown, as Dunphy and Jack going *mano-a-mano*.

There had been a press conference at which Dunphy would ask Jack a question: does Jack think that the team should play the same way in the finals of a major tournament as they did in qualifying? Jack refused to answer Dunphy's question, because he was not a 'proper journalist'. Which was about as good a result as Dunphy could get, in the circumstances.

The English journos saw Dunphy as a martyr for free speech and even the resentful Irish ones, the 'fans with typewriters', had to acknowledge that he was where he needed to be: front and centre. And they, the 'proper' journalists, were in the front row taking notes.

The Fear went on for a bit longer against Holland than against England, but again it was relatively short — after 17 minutes, Gullit scored, playing a one-two and finishing it into the bottom corner, like the superior being we knew him to be.

Holland had only managed a scoreless draw against England, so we figured they might take it out on us. But we weren't done yet. We could always rely on England to cheer us up, which they duly did by going ahead against Egypt, with a goal by centre-half Mark Wright.

We now had the additional stress of trying to work out the various permutations we needed to get ourselves out of this bloody Group F. With everyone on the same points and goal difference before the match, in one scenario all four teams could finish with an identical record, raising the appalling prospect of the drawing of lots to decide all four positions. Ah, it was a terrible strain on the brain.

But there was a modicum of relief in the thought that losing to Holland had none of the catastrophic connotations of losing to England — we had no 'history' with Wor Dutch, apart from the fact that they beat us in Euro 88 and went on to win it. But we didn't mind that. Mercifully they had been sated somewhat by that victory, because for the rest of the half and deep into the second half, they showed no desire to tear us apart, as was their natural right.

And then Packie did it again.

At around the same time in the match as he'd done against England, Packie gritted his teeth and sent up a high, lobbing, dropping ball.

This time there was another mis-cue from a defender and the ball squirted away towards the goal, where it was chased down by Niall Quinn, sliding and poking it past the keeper, van Breukelen.

Madness was now heaped upon madness, because the pandemonium which ensued was quickly followed by what looked like a gentleman's agreement between both sides, to settle for a draw. This was so deeply surreal, no-one had any recollection of seeing such a thing happening before on an international playing pitch in a competitive context. But there they were, Ireland and Holland, apparently not trying any more. And to heighten the surrealism, this cosy little arrangement was founded on the premise that England would continue to beat Egypt in their match, happening simultaneously.

Which doesn't seem like a very strong premise, all things considered.

And as for the moral dimension … it seemed as if football had thrown everything at us during the last ten days and now it was asking us to take a trip into the moral maze, which we flatly refused to do, because in this situation, we had no morals.

It is remarkable indeed, and perhaps a little troubling, just how insensitive we were to the sufferings of the Egyptians. As if they hadn't suffered, too. Had they not been through war, within living memory? Were they not an ancient and venerable culture which had given nearly as much to human civilisation as we had? And even if they had given nothing, did they deserve to get knocked out of the World Cup by this sort of blackguardism?

Unfortunately, by asking these questions, the Egyptians would be mistaking us for people who gave a fuck.

So secure were we in our sense of victimhood, we could not feel their pain.

We could not feel any of it. Not a twinge. And even if I am starting to feel just a small pang of remorse, twenty years on, to cure it, all I have to do is think of that piece written by Paul Howard about his pursuit of the accursed Nazare, the referee who did us down in Brussels. All I have to do, is think of the nine-year-old Dion Fanning tearing out that picture of Nazare from the Sunday paper, and ripping it up in disgust.

So there was no point telling us that the hearts of the Egyptian people were crying, as they watched their World Cup being taken away from them in such a cruel fashion. And there was definitely no point in telling Dion Fanning, that he should feel bad about anything, as he made his way to a party to celebrate with a house full of other young people who were already wildly drunk. The Leaving was still on. But Fanning recalls he had 'broken the back of it' at this stage — if indeed it wasn't already broken before that first English paper.

Arthur and Liam and I were getting a taxi from Dun Laoghaire into town, where we would be meeting Mr George Byrne in the Pink Elephant for drinks. Outside, it was Latin America, the horns blaring, flags flying out of cars, the 'Olé-Olé'-ing and the 'Give-It-A-Lash-Jack'-ing.

Unbelievably, there was still one more good thing to happen to us, one more break for us to catch. Tied on points and goal difference with Holland, we were awarded second place in the Group by the drawing of lots. Which meant that in the last 16, Holland got Germany.

All we had to do was to beat Romania.

Chapter 16 ～

| DRINKING IT ALL IN

'I missed the World Cup,' Con Houlihan mourned. 'I went to Italy.'

During Italia 90, families sat down together and made what they believed were rational decisions to spend the money they had been saving for years for an extension to the house, on this holiday in Italy. I was particularly impressed by the story of a man who 'bet' that Ireland would finish second in the Group, booking cheap accommodation well in advance for his family in Genoa for a match in the last 16 that might never happen — sensible people, living on the edge for a while.

But mostly, it was as sensible as it can ever be when a bunch of drunk lads gets into a mini-bus outside their local pub in the centre of Dublin, and sets off for the World Cup. For all their cavalier attitude, they would be humbled by legends of men who opted for some extremely complicated sea-route, because they just liked the idea of sailing to Sardinia in an extremely dangerous boat. Or the guy from Limerick who flew there and back in a single-engine aircraft, allegedly made from little more than plywood.

And all this, to miss the World Cup.

But we would hear of the adventures of the Green Army, mainly through the radio reports of Nell McCafferty for the Pat Kenny show. As a rule, I am fiercely opposed to journalists who don't know much about sport doing 'colour pieces', based on the flawed premise that they can bring a 'fresh perspective' to the occasion, can see things that maybe the more seasoned observers have stopped seeing.

In fact, they usually end up seeing very little that is of any interest to anyone, because there is some essential aspect of sport that eludes them, an obsessional quality without which sport itself is meaningless.

A big football match is not like the Spring Show with a slightly more competitive edge. It is not an 'occasion' in the usual sense — there is too much at stake, for the faithful. Of course, a lot of people have never felt that obsession, that intensity, but Italia 90 gave them a taste of it, a sense of what some of us had been feeling for most of our lives. And when it was over, they would never really feel it again.

So on the whole I would prefer not to hear reports by people who are coming to it with this 'fresh perspective', but in the case of Nell, I would make an exception. Nell is a great reporter, who works best when she is mingling with folks, just hearing their confessions, as it were. And as the Irish made their way towards Genoa, she was able to bring a genuinely fresh perspective and to muse on the meaning of it all.

Nell wouldn't see such an extraordinary journey in isolation from all the other extraordinary things that had been happening back home throughout the 1980s, all the sheer bloody unhappiness and unpleasantness which was now being purged on this weird odyssey. In particular she described what it meant for all these men and how they were behaving themselves so far away from home. Nell, the feminist, was impressed by a lot of what she saw, not least the fact that so few of them were screwing around, or even thinking about it. One fan, when in Rome and unable to find a hotel room, had had some sort of a sexual encounter with a Dutch woman in the catacombs. Happily married for five years, he felt the flagellations of guilt so well-known to Paddy in these situations, at home and abroad. And he went to Nell to confess. Seeing the state he was in, and the genuine agonies of conscience he was feeling, she told him to consider it a bonus and absolved him.

She noted that men who had never been on the continent before, were relishing the achievement of negotiating their way to Italy, and around Italy, and was particularly struck by one young man from one of the toughest parts of Dublin who had twelve different currencies in his possession, who had worked out a lot of things he never imagined he could work out and who broke away from the boys in Rome to take a trip to Pompeii, to broaden his mind.

Most memorable of all, were the scenes which reminded us that the Irish had no mobile phones then, that they really were on their own out there. So there would be a queue, a very long queue, outside a phone box. Mostly, they just wanted to tell the folks back home that they loved them.

At no other time, in Ireland or outside Ireland, have so many Irish people told other Irish people that they loved them. Paddy was liberated at this time, and not just by the drink. He had, after all, been drinking for quite a long time, without it coming to this. And in Italy with the heat and all the logistical issues, he couldn't drink like he could at home.

But the Italia 90 campaign gave him a new sort of confidence in certain areas. He didn't have to work out how to behave himself in front of all these foreigners. With the peer pressure and the reputation he had already garnered, he knew only one way to behave — he would behave well. That was all he needed to know. It could be reduced to a simple question and answer.

Q: How is he supposed to behave himself?

A: Well.

His normal levels of self-consciousness were heightened another few notches, but now he had these strong directions to guide him. To his antic disposition, was added a military discipline. And the mad uniform of the Green Army also gave him a certain camouflage, because it removed another area of doubt and confusion for Paddy, especially in a country such as Italy where they tend to be a bit on the stylish side. It meant he didn't have to be worrying about how he looked to the discerning eye. He was wearing an eejit's costume, which sent out the signal: this is an eejit's costume. It's not me.

It certain rare cases, of course, it might be an eejit's costume, containing an eejit.

But how could anyone tell?

———

Back home, we were also living in a strange country, perhaps all the stranger because we hadn't physically left the island. It felt as if we were living at altitude, as if all the best energies of the people directed towards the same cause had lightened the air itself.

We had come through these trials like the heroes of a medieval saga, and we were better people for it. What was the worst that could happen to us now? A big performance by Gheorghe Hagi, the Romanian captain, perhaps, but that was OK. We could live with Romania beating us, the same boys who used to come over here for 'the bit of freedom and some decent food'.

And we could enjoy the rest of the World Cup, as we became more accustomed to the notion that we were part of this — no less than the trees and the stars, we had a right to be here.

We could savour the last-16 match between Germany and Holland in particular, knowing that it could have been us out there, trying to beat the Germans. We knew the joke that football is a game played with a round ball by two teams, each of which contains eleven players, and in the end the Germans win.

———

It was the eve of our match against Romania, and we were drinking it all in.

The Romanians did not have the aura of the Germans or the Dutch, to overpower us.

Dunphy was back from Italy, his reputation secure.

Whatever about the best supporters in the world, we have always had the best TV panellists in the world, in Giles and Dunphy.

In fact, with his first-rate mind, cutting to the essence of any proposition, sensing the unmistakeable waft of bullshit a million miles away, Giles is probably the best TV analyst pound for pound across all areas, from politics to the arts to his own discipline, the one that matters. And his presence on the panel at this time was given further gravitas by all he had done for Ireland in the bad years, as player and manager, and all that had been done to him.

Dunphy always deferred to Giles as the better player and the better man, but Dunphy was now on a personal high, and loving it, baby!

He made an outstanding contribution to Germany v Holland in the second round when he analysed a spitting incident involving Frank Rijkaard and Rudi Voller, a scene which bespoke the terrible hatred which exists between these two nations. Using the magic pencil with which Giles would deconstruct a move, Dunphy drew a line from Rijkaard's gob to Voller's head, tracing the trajectory of the phlegm. Bill O'Herlihy watched indulgently, knowing he was in the presence of a master.

I was watching this in Smyth's pub in Dun Laoghaire, where I would sometimes run into Donagh Deeney, the Furniture Removal Man in *Juno* whom you may remember from Mulligan's of Manhattan, and Euro 88.

Ah, it was all coming together.

Germany won 2-1, confirming our suspicion that we had dodged another bullet there.

And the day after tomorrow, we would have the exceptional pleasure of watching England playing Cameroon, with the genuine prospect that the rampaging Africans would get a big, big result — shops in Dublin were selling out of Cameroon jerseys; we could feel it coming.

But the next day, it was Ireland v Romania in Genoa in the last 16 of the World Cup.

———

The International Bar, if it was so inclined, could probably claim that in the late 1980s it was the equivalent of McDaid's in the 1950s — the pub of choice of creative individuals who would achieve renown in the fullness of time, or even posthumously, but who were just starting out back then, or struggling. And who could get their cheques cashed by the barman, because they weren't particularly welcome in banks and because the amounts were usually small.

In fact, the reputation of McDaid's is based mainly on its association with literary men such as Brendan Behan, Patrick Kavanagh, Flann O'Brien, Anthony Cronin, and J.P. Donleavy, whereas the International was a haven for all sorts. Virtually every Irish comedian of the time, several of whom became internationally successful, started out upstairs in the International. From Ardal O'Hanlon to Dylan Moran to Tommy Tiernan to Deirdre O'Kane to Kevin Gildea to Des Bishop to Barry Murphy, they would stand up in the Comedy Cellar and sit down afterwards in the main bar, which felt like a place of worship to the great god of alcohol, an altar. Or they would hide downstairs in the womb-like comfort of the basement lounge.

Conor McPherson put on some of his early work in the International. Members of the Rough Magic theatre company, such as Declan Hughes, the playwright and novelist and Lynne Parker, the director, were there or thereabouts. I remember Anne Enright, who was then working in RTÉ on the *Nighthawks* show, meeting Graham Linehan in the downstairs lounge to talk about something he had written or wanted to write for the programme, which itself was doing something different by being on RTÉ and being consistently funny, with Kevin McAleer in particular nailing the deep strangeness of Paddy's eclectic cultural life.

And just in passing, Shay Healy's *Nighthawks* interview with Sean Doherty brought down Charles J. Haughey.

————

Anne Enright would eventually win the Booker Prize and Graham Linehan would win BAFTA awards, though at the time, if you could have imagined such an astonishing thing, you might have assumed it would be the other way round — Enright, after all, was working in television at the time, while Linehan had not yet gone there, and seemed bright enough to write anything he wanted to write.

And so the International could claim that it provided all these talented young people with a University-of-Life education which enabled them to rule the world. Except it didn't really feel like that.

In fact, the whole point of the International was that it was so unassuming, so lacking any of that bullshit. Most of the clientele and the performers upstairs would be dealing with Simon the Wicklow barman, a thoroughly sound man, a kindly individual from another age who cycled into work every day and who may have been the least arty-farty man in Ireland at that time. Apart perhaps from Matt, the other barman.

And though you could compile an impressive list of notable individuals who drank there, they weren't all drinking there on the same nights, and many of them probably never believed they would go as far as they did — in fact for much of the 1980s most of them probably thought they were going nowhere. I don't think that John Waters secretly saw himself selling about 40,000 copies of his first book, *Jiving at the Crossroads* and I doubt that Fiona Looney had an unspoken belief that her first play, *Dandelions*, would become one the most successful theatrical productions of all time in this country.

And did a later *Hot Press*er Peter Murphy imagine that he would write the novel *John The Revelator*, which would be described by Roddy Doyle as 'like reading for the first time, almost as if I'd never read a novel before'?

I don't think so.

There wouldn't be enough drink in the world to make all that seem possible.

——

Looking back, it seems crazy that Conor McPherson could make that journey from lunchtime in the International to a run on Broadway. But as usual we must turn to football to give us a proper understanding of the nature of success on this scale and what it means. Because the breakthroughs of various individuals in the arts and show business were mirrored on a gigantic scale by the success of the Republic.

Whether these individuals would be inspired by the success of the football team, we can only guess — in fact, I know that Graham Linehan was almost totally uninspired by anything to do with football, and Arthur was funny long before we qualified for Euro 88 — but you could make a case that goes something like this: that breakthrough which the Republic made, which we thought would never happen until it actually did, gave everyone in Ireland an inkling of what success feels like, how exhilarating it can be. And because so many of us felt it and felt a part of it, we probably became more comfortable with the idea of success as a result, warily casting aside the culture of failure in which we had wallowed for so long.

In the years that followed, when we saw someone doing well for himself, even if we couldn't relate to what he was doing, we knew how he felt, in some small way, because we had all been there, for a few moments, during Italia 90.

And we all understood, too, as never before, what a thin line it is between the crushing weight of disappointment and that surge of endorphins you get when you're winning. Against Romania in the last 16, that line was so thin, there was nothing in it for ninety minutes and nothing in it for another half-hour of extra time and eventually there was nothing in it but a penalty kick.

———

It had to be the International, for this one, Liam and Arthur and George Byrne and I emerging again from the sanctuary of our homes to the relative sanctuary of our home away from home — it meant we could partake of the community spirit while still drawing solace from these so-familiar surroundings, sitting up at the marbled counter with the telly in the top right-hand corner where Gary Mackay had scored for Scotland, and with Simon manning the pumps.

The fact that we had a stool at the counter indicates that we got there early doors, to acclimatise, quite an achievement in itself on this day when no-one in Ireland was even pretending that a day's work would be done. As if watching Ireland v Romania playing for a place in the quarter-final of the World Cup wasn't work. And all the drinking that had to be done to make it even vaguely bearable could hardly be classed as anything but work, and essential work. There may have been a few people left in the country who regarded football at this level as a leisure pursuit, but for the overwhelming majority, until the result was known, this would be a day of agonising toil.

They were three or four deep at the bar of the International by kick-off, and those of us who were fortunate to have a seat were un-fortunate in having to lift pints back through the crowd.

The match itself was a disgrace, another 90 minutes and another 30 minutes on top of that with almost no football being played, apart from the odd little spasm by the Romanians, who then seemed to concede that they were only codding themselves trying to play football against the likes of us. Even with the Berlin Wall down, those boys from Eastern Europe didn't need much persuading that the cynical option was the best, that you might as well play for penalties if they're offered to you.

And though there was this underlying sense of inevitability that we would end up in a penalty shoot-out, it did not lessen the Fear in any way.

You could never entirely trust those Romanians to go with the flow, not with Hagi lurking there, a deeply troubling presence.

As for us, we had sort of got out of the habit of winning football matches, in the accepted sense. In the Compromise Rules format which we were perfecting, we favoured this idea of getting a draw in such a way that it felt like a win. It was the smart response to that inherent design flaw of the system — that it was now very difficult for the other team to score goals, but it was just as difficult for us to score goals. In fact, if you reminded a lot of folks that we hadn't actually *won* the games against England and Holland, they would have given you a funny look.

So with all the conviction that Jack had drummed into them, the lads had eventually imposed their will on the opposition, so that in Genoa, the Romanians ended up playing us at our own game — playing for the draw and getting it.

The great moments are known to all — Packie's save and his leap into immortality, George Hamilton bellowing, 'The nation holds its breath!', the entire squad running to acclaim David O'Leary, RTÉ's Bill O'Herlihy putting on a stupid hat with clapping hands on top, the TV pictures of the uncontrolled weeping of John Healy at the EU summit which was happening around the corner from the International in Dublin Castle, Healy the reporter who had written the most poignant lament for Paddy at his lowest moment in the 1950s, when no-one shouted stop.

Perhaps it was racing through Healy's mind that the emigration which had torn the heart out of the country had somehow given us back a decent football team and brought us to this, forty years later.

In the International we had entered some demented realm of magic realism. I looked behind me at a wall of people going mad with joy and one of them just happened to be a guy who had grown up a short distance away from me in Athlone, a brilliant guitar player called Anthony Stapleton with whom I had played football on an under-12 team. We had been cheated out of a place in the final of a local tournament by bad refereeing, which was one of the first really horrible things that happened to me in my life and which possibly scars me still. And now here was Anthony in the International, the two of us roaring at one another.

And then he was gone.

There was something so strange about this, I would prefer not to dwell on it.

Strange too, that when O'Leary was announced as the next penalty taker, an inner voice told me that he would probably score, because I had this clear memory of him taking a few penalties for the Arsenal. It was only much later that I was told that O'Leary had never taken a penalty in his life.

I have no idea where that voice came from, telling me of O'Leary's expertise in dead-ball situations, but I suspect it may have been the baleful gods taking pity on me, feeding me this false information to curb my anxiety. Or maybe it was just the drink.

And there was that image of Jack during the shoot-out, apparently in a state of total relaxation. Which could either mean that he was showing exemplary leadership as usual, exuding this sense of inner calm which would be transmitted to his men and make all the difference, or that he really was completely relaxed because the job was done — whether we won the penalties or lost the penalties, by not getting beaten at this stage of the tournament, it was now established as indisputable fact that we had not been disgraced.

Ah, he was so like us, in so many ways.

I remember him declining to say 'An Bord Gáis', which he insisted on calling 'the gas board'. They could have told him to just pronounce it *Un Board Gosh*, and maybe they did, but Jack would prefer to do it the way he wanted it, the way which made him comfortable, rather than run even the smallest risk of embarrassment.

He was so like us, the way we shudder when we see one of our own on the BBC, fearing that they will embarrass themselves and embarrass us in front of our mammies and daddies, the Brits.

To avoid embarrassment — with Jack, as with Paddy, this was a holy thing.

Down, down we went to the basement lounge of the International, at that point of perfect happiness with the victory over Romania still vibrating inside us and the prospect of the quarter-final against Italy in the Stadio Olimpico a serene and beautiful vision.

Standing at the bar, waiting for another drink, I was seized by the urge to slam my fist down on the counter, at the good of it all. I had never before slammed my fist on anything, either in joy or in sorrow — I was not a fist-slamming sort of guy — but there I was, slamming my fist on the counter.

Simon, who was busy filling pints, simply smiled.

There is a story from this time of a man — we'll call him Kevin — in another bar, Fitzgerald's of Sandycove. Kevin's wife was at home in an advanced state of pregnancy. Her friend rang the pub to say that his wife had gone into labour, the contractions had started. 'Tell her I'll be up when the penos are finished,' he said.

When Kevin eventually made it home, his wife was in an even more advanced state of pregnancy. He sat in an armchair, while his wife counted between contractions. Then, overcome by the day's exertions, he fell fast asleep.

By the time his wife woke him up to drive her to the hospital, the streets were full of wild people, singing and dancing. Kevin had the window of the car rolled down and was shaking hands with other fans. People were dancing on the bonnet of the car.

'For Christ's sake will you get them lunatics off the car and get me to hospital', his wife screamed at him.

Kevin was feeling a riot of emotion. Torn between his elation at the result and the distressing condition of his wife, he drove as best he could through the open-air madhouse which the city had become.

In the back his wife was now weeping with agony.

Observing the scenes of great joy through which they were moving, he tried to comfort her with soothing words like, 'Where would you get it, eh?'

But her weeping only became more intense. At which point a large beery man, seeing her weeping, stuck his head through the window, and offered her these words of consolation: 'Ah jaysus, Missus, I know how you feel, I shed a few tears meself earlier on.'

| NO REGRETS

The psychologists would probably tell you that we didn't have a chance against Italy.

They'd say that you have to be able to visualise yourself winning. You have to genuinely believe you can do it. And of course you have to want it and need it, with every fibre of your being. They would say that we had already got what we wanted. In fact, they would say that we had got more than we wanted, more than we could ever have visualised ourselves getting.

And they would probably be right. In the case of Jack, they would certainly be right.

Jack was just not the sort of fellow to indulge in flights of fancy: such things were not just foolish, they were unprofessional. In fact, the further we got in the competition, the greater the risk that he would find himself re-living the latter part of his playing career with Leeds, challenging for the game's most glorious honours and castigating himself for getting into all that hassle: 'How do we do it?'

Getting the job done … achieving what you set out to achieve … such an uncomplicated approach had got us to the last 16 of the World Cup. Getting to the quarter-final was just a supremely happy accident. And in truth, most of us would have had that attitude. Looking back at what was a very bad World Cup in general, in terms of the quality of the football, you might say that we weren't greedy enough.

And maybe some of us learned our lesson and decided in the years to come that we could never be accused of that again.

But for now, we were sated. We didn't want it all, because deep down, we felt that we already had it all.

Not that we didn't want to beat Italy. In fact, so many wondrous things had been happening, we were prepared to entertain that fantasy, too. And even to imagine that the movie mightn't end there, that we might end up playing England in the World Cup Final, England who just happened to be in the other half of the draw.

So maybe we wanted it, but the shrinks would say that we didn't want it enough. And we would all probably accept that we didn't need it. As a small country, we had got so much out of this so far. We had satisfied all the football needs we ever had and a few more we never knew we had.

At this stage of the tournament the bigger countries started to need it more. Germany needed it: just to ensure a decent welcome home, they needed to win the World Cup. Argentina needed it, even though they had won it the last time. England needed it, but were never going to get it. Maybe even Cameroon needed it more than we did — the ageless Roger Milla with his four goals and his dancing at the corner-flag seemed capable of anything.

Italy most certainly needed it. And they must have looked benignly at our lads on their big day out, having an audience with the Pope. Not unfamiliar themselves with the traditions of Roman Catholicism, they would know that an audience with the Pope is something of a crowning glory, something you tend to get when you have already accomplished something, such, as, say, winning the World Cup.

Certainly the Italian team wouldn't be heading over to the Vatican in this fashion without the trophy. And it may have crossed their minds that the Irish were doing it at this stage, because when the Pope had his audience the following week, they wouldn't be around.

Perhaps it was this sense of an achievement being honoured which made us all take such a benign attitude to this audience with the Pope. Because lest we forget, in Ireland we had just spent most of the decade embroiled in a sort of a religious war, in which one side was vehemently opposed to the power still being wielded and abused by said Pope and his minions.

If you wanted to be pedantic about it, you could say that the 'diaspora', which was so well represented by Jack's squad, had contained an awful lot of unfortunate women who had to leave Ireland to have their illegitimate children in England, spurned by a fearful nation which was taking its orders directly from Rome.

In fact, that would not be pedantic, it would just be true.

But the magic of Italia 90 was working here too, allowing us to leave aside our ideological differences and to look at this in the best possible light.

We would forgive the fact that the last time we saw John Paul II among the Irish, he was using Father Michael Cleary as his warm-up man. We would forget all the irreversible damage done to us by what could broadly be termed 'Catholic teaching'. We would rise above our reasoned arguments and see this instead as an emotional rather than a religious event, acknowledging that ours had been a deeply Catholic country, in which many would see this as the ultimate honour, and they, too, have their story.

And we would observe that John Paul II had something which was lacking in most of Official Ireland, and Official Italy for that matter — a genuine love of football.

We would see the deep devotion of men such as physio Mick Byrne, for whom this would be a great and solemn ceremony.

We first encountered Mick back at the airport hotel, during that interview with Jack for *Hot Press*, the one in which Jack called for draconian measures to be taken in the light of the growing environmental scandal of fish-kills caused by slurry being emptied into rivers and lakes. But I had encountered Mick much earlier in my life, watching him scuttling across the muck of St Mel's Park with his bag of tricks, to treat the injuries of Athlone Town players.

Even as The Town's physio he cut a most striking figure, as he was clearly fitter than any of the players. And with his evident sincerity, his fierce loyalty to the cause of Ireland, he had now become a 'character' in the Charlton story, and a much-loved one. No-one in his right mind would begrudge Mick Byrne his precious moments in the presence of the Pope.

But according to legend, his experience at Italia 90 was not entirely an uplifting one. There is a story told in Andy Townsend's autobiography, *Andy's Game* (written with Paul Kimmage) of a scene which unfolded in the foyer of the hotel in Palermo where the Irish squad was staying before the Egypt match, a scene which allegedly unfolded as follows:

The hotel was quite a modest, family-run operation, and some of the players were becoming increasingly bored. So it happened that players such as Townsend and Tony Cascarino were lounging around the foyer of this hotel, with nothing to engage them except superb models of ships mounted on plinths, which the owner of the hotel had apparently assembled himself, using millions of matchsticks. These ships were the great work of his life.

Seeing the lads so bored, a passing Mick Byrne felt that they needed a bit of diversion. Putting on his best Cockney accent, he began to sing and perform a version of 'The Lambeth Walk' for them, there in the foyer. Which they were enjoying, up to a point. They said nothing about it, but they couldn't help noticing that he was getting so involved in the performance, walking backwards and forwards, that he was getting dangerously close at times to the model ships.

Too close, indeed.

Catastrophically close, as he bumped into one of them, and the whole damn thing was overturned during a climactic moment of the song.

Despite the desperate efforts of Byrne to catch the falling object, the great ship was destroyed.

As he surveyed the wreckage, they say that Byrne's face was a vision of utter mortification. And then the owner of the hotel, hearing the commotion, burst through the door, to see his beloved matchstick masterpiece lying in ruins. He was screaming in Italian. He was inconsolable. Mick Byrne could only keep repeating his apologies, crucified with shame.

For the footballers who had witnessed the accident, there was only one possible response to this developing crisis — helpless, uncontrollable laughter. In fact, they were laughing so hard, as a thorough professional it may have momentarily occurred to Mick Byrne that they might do themselves an injury here.

But he would have to deal with that another time, as the owner's wife had now arrived and was equally apoplectic.

'I'm sorry, I'm really sorry,' Mick repeated, as abjectly apologetic as it is possible for any man to be, talking to a stranger in a foreign language.

But then apparently a change started to come over him, because so unforgiving were the owner and his wife, so relentless their wailing and gnashing of teeth, that after about five minutes of this they set something off in the too-noble heart of Mick Byrne. It seems they pushed him over the edge, into anger.

'I no sorry with you any more,' he said, a new note of defiance in his voice.

And he left them with this: 'Fuck you, and fuck your boat.'

———

No psychologist could have relaxed the lads any better than Mick Byrne doing the Lambeth Walk. But it obviously hadn't worked in Palermo.

We tried to tell ourselves that the total lack of expectation, the very fact that we didn't need anything else from them, that they owed us nothing at this stage, would perversely bring the best out of the team on the Saturday night in Rome.

George Byrne was in the International on the Friday night when he got a call on the pay-phone from the *Hot Press* — there was a ticket available for Rome and the Stadio Olimpico, did he want to go? Thus George was at Busarus early next morning, getting the bus out to the airport. An elderly woman put her head around the door and spoke to the driver:

'Is this the bus to Lough Derg?' she asked.

As Father Trendy might have put it: 'And you know, in a way … it was'.

That lady may well have been the only living Irish person who was thinking about anything except Italy versus Ireland, though the actor Michael James Ford recalls that the Gate Theatre, perhaps taking its spirit of independence a step too far, stayed open that night for its production of Steven Berkoff's *Salome*, with cast and crew preoccupied by events in Rome, and an audience with no Irish people in it, just a party of about 40 slightly bewildered American tourists.

But again the head-shrinkers would find it revealing that for many of us, this was going to be something of a family occasion. I had decided to watch this at home, with Jane and Roseanne, who was now wearing a tiny green Ireland shirt. Looking back, it seems like one of those old photographs from the Second World War, in which the family gathers around the wireless to listen intently to some news of vast importance, concerning the fate of the nation and of the world. No doubt there was a feeling that this was an occasion of such magnitude in the history of Ireland, we would have to experience it together, as a family. It didn't really occur to me at the time, that there was a tacit acknowledgment here, that the war was over. That literally, we were all going home. That the time had come to return from the front to our loved ones.

Because football, at least if it's being done properly, is just not a form of family entertainment. The reasons are hard to define, but I guess there is just too much rage in it, too much inexplicable grief to be inflicting on the little ones.

It is not like rugby, where you can see the ladies of Munster at the airport bound for London or Paris to support the guys (always 'the guys', never the lads or the fellows, an iron-clad class distinction there) looking forward to a wonderful weekend away, wining and dining and maybe taking in a show. Rugby doesn't really matter. It doesn't matter to the multitudes and it doesn't even matter a great deal to the aficionados, who are never down for too long after a defeat, because in the end they are all winners, all on the same side, with the upper middle classes, against the common good.

And as for the Official Irelanders who came to the party around the time of Jack, football matters in a way that they do not understand, these dilettantes, these bandwagon-jumpers, these corporate swine.

It is a thing of appalling intensity, a primal thing, at once both an individual and a tribal obsession. And somehow, along with all this borderline savagery, it is also beautiful. Albert Camus knew this, with his line that everything he knew most surely about morality and obligations he had learned from football, and Eamon Dunphy, who would often quote Camus, knew it too.

So, as he sat in the Stadio Olimpico, watching Ireland going down 1-0, Dunphy was having none of this all-of-Ireland-in-it-together shit. If you want family entertainment, you should check out Des O'Connor, baby! Dunphy lashed out a piece for the front page of the *Sunday Independent* which revisited his familiar themes — the betrayal of the finer traditions of Irish football by this caveman attitude, the misuse by Jack of the talent at his disposal which, in better hands, might have taken us all the way.

Out on the running track, various other significant figures in Irish life were making their contribution to the night, adding touches of surrealism which could only come from Paddy operating at full throttle. For a start there was the surrealism of this unrestrained celebration, after what had been a fairly comfortable win for Italy. For Jack, waving his tricolour, there was perhaps a touch of relief to be going home. For everyone, indeed, there was maybe this feeling of relief that it was all over now, and this was the worst that had happened to us, a defeat by the narrowest margin by the host nation.

Charlie Haughey was out there joining in the celebrations, and so was Chris de Burgh.

Perhaps predictably, people asked what the fuck Chris de Burgh was doing out there, but in fact, Chris de Burgh probably had more of a right to be out there than Haughey. Chris de Burgh is a genuine football fan, a supporter of Liverpool FC: indeed, when full-back Markus Babbel was struck down by a debilitating virus, de Burgh made a personal intervention, attempting to heal him with his powers.

He did not succeed. But he meant well.

And in Rome, he had entertained the team in their hotel, which helps to explain why he had access all areas. It fact, it is not beyond the bounds of possibility that Chris was going to see the Republic long before he was in a position to get there in a private jet.

Haughey never gave a tuppenny damn about football, though in the heat of that Italian summer night, no-one would be reminding us of those invitations to Lansdowne Road from the FAI, which he had ignored. Some will say that this is what makes us unique, that it is impossible to imagine the Prime Minister of any other country in the world joining the celebrations in this way, out on the running track, again leaving aside the minor detail that there was ostensibly nothing to be celebrating.

And maybe it is a good thing that our leader would do this, and the British Prime Minister wouldn't. In fact, it would be hard to imagine the leader of Togo out there, with Togo's leading balladeer in close attendance.

It seems that Paddy is always destined to be the mad fella — even at the biggest party with an international guest-list, he will insist on it.

And it would be a good thing — in fact it would be a great thing — if this willingness of the Taoiseach to get down with the people was part of a broader story of sporting ambition, with the government backing all sorts of sporting endeavours and rightly taking the credit for it.

But it wasn't quite like that, in 1990.

For example, there was no 50-metre swimming pool in Ireland at that time, nor were there any plans to build one. There was hardly even a running track. And you don't really need to know much more than that, to form a view of Official Ireland's commitment to sport, and Haughey's entitlement to the cheers of the Green Army, on that night.

In Togo, they'd probably got around to building a pool, and maybe even filling it with water, some time back in the 1970s. But not in Ireland.

Still, it somehow suited our idea of life as a cabaret, to have Haughey there taking his bow at Italia 90, just as he materialised for Stephen Roche on the podium at the Tour de France.

Even Berlusconi, a man with no limits, who had contributed some of his own money to the betterment of football in his country, would not be seen celebrating on the pitch with the Azzurri when they actually won the World Cup in Germany.

But that night in the Stadio Olimpico, we wound it all up with something akin to an open-air episode of the *Late Late Show* — a bit of Jack and the Boys In Green, a bit of Chris de Burgh, a bit of Haughey, even a bit of Dunphy. And with the best wishes of the Pope still with us, a little bit of religion. And the entire country — and for once we literally meant the entire country, every man, woman and child — watching it.

And Liam Brady watching it too, in his street clothes.

Ah, it was not right, in so many ways, and yet it still felt good to see us there, for once in our lives. It felt good to see Paul McGrath out there, with the world watching, displaying in one movement down the right and a cross to the head of Niall Quinn, why we deserved to be there, for him if for no other reason.

But Walter Zenga saved the header, and we didn't trouble him much after that.

Deep down we felt that maybe Packie could have done better with that shot from Donadoni, that he could have palmed it wide or over the bar or anywhere except straight to Totò Schillaci, who was on fire.

But we just don't have enough heroes to be casting them aside for one debatable indiscretion. And anyway, as a few more of us were starting to understand, that's football.

You could even see a certain maturity in all this, in the way we were able to listen to what Dunphy was saying, and know there was something in it, and still give the lads the most massive homecoming in Dublin on the day after they got knocked out. We had reached the last eight of the World Cup at our first attempt, and yet on the front page of the biggest Sunday paper we were reading a lament.

And for that, Paddy can feel just a bit grown-up.

Not that he would sit with that feeling for too long. There would be a homecoming, with Jack becoming increasingly and understandably terrified that the children running alongside the bus would be killed. But there was also the matter of England v Cameroon in the quarter-final.

There was still something in it for us, even on the day after we were finished.

———

The prospect of Cameroon and England was like waking up with a hangover after a party to realise another session has started in the pub up the road, and they're asking for you.

RTÉ was still remarkably doing the right thing, covering the homecoming live, in its entirety. There are men of my acquaintance, hardened journalists, who have been known to watch this on video after a few drinks and to have a good cry — though on the subject of crying, in the context of Italia 90, Jimmy Rabbitte in Roddy Doyle's *The Snapper* has this to say: 'drunk doesn't count'.

And perhaps it is right that the players had the best view on the flight from Rome, when the pilot changed direction over Dublin to show them the scene down below, the throngs that were waiting for them when they got off the plane, which had been named Saint Jack.

They would be welcomed by Mr Haughey, who had arrived home before them, and they would be taken by open-topped bus from the airport to O'Connell Street, the same street that had been entirely deserted in the middle of the afternoon for the Romania match, resulting in astonishing pictures in the papers of the city's main thoroughfare looking like the set of *High Noon* before the shooting started.

For the homecoming, it was estimated that 300,000 had gathered in or around O'Connell Street, while about 50,000 Germans turned out to hail the new World Champions — we should mention in passing that Germany would beat Argentina 1-0 in the final, a predictably poor game settled by a penalty, confirming the fact that whilst all World Cups should be held in Italy, the next time it would be nice to see some football as well.

Did Argentina morally deserve to win because of the way Maradona had been kicked and kicked and kicked again by every member of every team who encountered him? No, they had black-heartedly played for penalties like the lowest of them.

RTÉ kept winning all the way. There was even reason to believe that Montrose had been seized by the spirit of the BBC in the glory days, when they put together a sequence of the Republic's highlights matched with Edith Piaf singing 'No Regrets'. For Paddy to have been on the ran-tan for a month solid, at home and abroad, and to be able to say with some sincerity that he had no regrets, was astonishing.

The highlights package, of course, was not exactly as aesthetically pleasing as Carlos Alberto scoring the fourth goal for Brazil in the Azteca Stadium in 1970 — it was mostly Packie hoofing them up and keeping them out — but the indomitable spirit of Piaf seemed to merge with the indomitable spirit of Paddy, to produce an emotional *tour de force*.

And Nelson Mandela, the most indomitable of them all, just happened to be receiving the Freedom of Dublin on the afternoon of the homecoming.

It had been awarded to him in 1988 when he did not even have the freedom of Robben Island, a gesture which reflected all the fun we had had in the 1980s, going to gigs the proceeds of which would go to the Anti-Apartheid movement. Or perhaps dancing in Leeson Street clubs with a few bottles of red inside us, to the sounds of 'Free Nelson Mandela' by Special AKA — yes, we all did what we could.

But there was a man who was on the plane home from Italy, one of the Boys In Green, who had made an actual contribution. The full-back Chris Hughton had been one of ten sportsmen that Mandela had asked to meet on his release, to convey his appreciation of the good work they had done, over the years — Chris was wearing a Mandela T-shirt on the day we spoke to him in Windmill Lane, on the day of the recording of the anthem for Euro 88.

But he had done more than wear the T-shirt. And Mandela wanted to meet him. Seeing as the two men were going to be in town on the same day, strenuous efforts were made by activists such as Kader Asmal of the Anti-Apartheid movement, to bring Hughton and Mandela together. But with the flight from Italy delayed, and with the vastness of the crowds, it didn't happen.

So on this day of liberation, the honouring of Mandela at the

Mansion House became a sort of a warm-up for the civic reception that would happen later at the Bank of Ireland in College Green, 'Ooh-aah-Paul-McGrath's-Da', the crowd would chant, paying Mandela the highest compliment they could bestow.

We were in a very good place that day, human kindness over-flowing.

And now, were the Indomitable Lions of the Cameroon going to give us one for the road?

They were playing England that night in Naples, in the quarter-final.

The first African team to qualify for the quarter-final of a World Cup had played with an exuberance which had brought them red and yellow cards, while England were looking a good bet to win the Fair Play award, perhaps the only trophy they would take home.

It was probably the best football match of the tournament, if you were interested in that sort of thing. Cameroon were taking England apart at times, the commentators delighting Paddy with obser-vations that all the sophisticated stuff was being played by the men in green, while the stolid journeymen of England, playing their Third-World standard of football, tried to hang on somehow.

With about eight minutes to go the Indomitable Lions were leading the Three Lions 2-1. Then a bit of 'naïve' defending — naïve being the racist code for 'wild', 'undisciplined', 'typically African' — sent Lineker flying and with a degree of composure which in another context might be regarded as admirable, he stuck away the equaliser. He did the same thing in extra time.

And though all of Ireland mourned, yet again we were comforted by the thought that there is always someone worse off than our-selves, in this case the unfortunate people of Cameroon, who must have been gutted to lose like this. What was it like to boss the game as they had done, to play the champagne football, and to be going home anyway? We would never know such grief, but we were saddened enough to see England in the semi-final, though it raised a familiar dilemma for us — given our voracious interest in them, we needed them to qualify for major tournaments and to go as far as possible in them to sustain that interest of ours.

So, perversely, by staying alive in Italia 90, they were also keeping it alive for us. They were making it possible for us to squeeze a few more sparks out of it.

We would not rest until we knew their fate.

It would not entirely ruin it for us, if they went and won it, but it would challenge us. And Paddy doesn't really like a challenge, in that sense.

By now we were well aware that, when they weren't supporting us, the English were actually feeling quite enthusiastic about their own team, and enjoying Italia 90 with at least some of the fervour that we had shown.

But apart from their best wishes, they had one more gift for us. They gave us another great defeat, against the Germans in the semi-final in Turin, with Gazza weeping and the one he called The Waddler blasting that last spot-kick over the bar.

Then, and only then, were we ready for Pavarotti.

Chapter 18 ~

| THE FAT MAN SINGS

W
e can debate the pivotal nature of that period in Ireland, the tipping points; we can argue about the knock-on effects of Italia 90 on various aspects of Irish life, its influence on our psychology, our philosophy, our prosperity and our way of being in the world. But the one thing we know for sure is that the Three Tenors concert started something that is still with us today and will probably be with us for the foreseeable future. Luciano Pavarotti, Placido Domingo and José Carreras, singing in the ruins of the Baths of Caracalla on the eve of the Final of Italia 90, can be held directly responsible for much that followed in Ireland in the three-tenors genre.

At the time of writing, it is estimated that there are approximately 459 groups of men, three in number, with tenor voices of the Irish variety, going around calling themselves The Three Irish Tenors, or the Three Tenors from Ireland, or Ireland's Three Tenors or Tenors of Ireland Three, as well as peculiar off-shoots such as The Priests, doubtless spawning The Three Irish Priests, Three Priests from Ireland and so on forever.

But it seemed like a swell idea at the time.

If we must listen to three tenors, let it be these three tenors, in a glorious Italian setting. With the orchestra, conducted by Zubin Mehta, last seen waving the baton in front of the New York Philharmonic, playing 'Rhapsody In Blue'.

Pavarotti had already had a good World Cup, with 'Nessun Dorma'.

What we didn't quite realise, on the night, was that this would become a new form of corporate entertainment, from which not even Paddy would be exempt — on the contrary, he would take it and make it his own. When you think about it, opera singers had been doing a form of corporate entertainment for years before the concept was officially named. Indeed, opera is the perfect form of corporate entertainment — it has high-class connotations to those who don't know any better; it is mostly in a foreign language so it's all right if you don't have a clue what's going on; it is ridiculously expensive; and you're only allowed in if you're dressed respectably.

And now it was associating itself with sport, making it irresistible to the corporate sector and greatly assisting in the creation of a toxic sub-culture that is still with us.

The Three Tenors on the night were a novelty and they gave big performances but even against that fabulous backdrop of ancient Rome, there were moments when you could see how this thing could turn ugly, in the wrong hands.

They were doing 'operatic' versions of songs from *West Side Story* which merely confirmed that the original 'American' versions were innately superior, that pop music had for long been the greater art form, and that this 'high-class' stuff had become music for people who don't really like music — the fur coat brigade who can other-wise be found in the theatre on opening nights. They were all there in the crowd, these well-dressed barbarians, many of them doubtless believing that they were raising the tone of what had otherwise been a vulgar festival.

We remembered that Placido Domingo had made an album with John Denver and we figured that these were the people who bought it, as company for their other two albums. Pavarotti would work with artists of a higher calibre, such as Elton John, and there was always a certain grandeur about anything he did. But for all their vocal gymnastics, he and his cohorts took corporate entertainment to a new level that night in the Baths of Caracalla, and for that they must be condemned.

The corporate sector was moving in on sport in general in a big way by this stage, and particularly on football. By the time of the opening match of the 1998 World Cup in Paris, commentators would be remarking that there was no atmosphere in the ground, apparently unaware that there were hardly any people at these showpiece events any more, just well-lunched executives with free tickets.

And the new kid in town, Corporate Paddy, was watching too. With interest.

We started out with Christy Moore in *Time* magazine, now Paddy was grasping the other end of it, maybe the wrong end of it, and making his way towards *Forbes* magazine. Those fabled flights to Rome, in which everyone who was anyone tried to get to the Stadio Olimpico for the quarter-final, was perhaps the first ostentatious flexing of Paddy's corporate muscle.

It wasn't quite what we had envisaged, on those endless nights at the *Hot Press*. Remembering how we had felt about things back then, John Waters described it to me like this: 'We probably wouldn't have been able to tell you exactly what we wanted,' he said. 'But if you'd presented us with some putative outcome, we'd certainly have been able to tell you whether it fitted in to that picture. And what you can say for certain about what happened from 1990 onwards, is that it wasn't what we wanted. In fact, it had almost nothing of what we wanted in it.'

Our rich people were really getting off on the Boys In Green. Arnold O'Byrne had company now, 'putting de boot in', and those guys love making analogies between football and what they do. Even if what they do is selling pensions, they like to think it is not dissimilar in certain ways to what Totò Schillaci was doing.

So they came on board in a big way towards the end of Italia 90, and thereafter they would be seen supporting the lads from the good seats in Wembley, at the Giants Stadium, wherever they felt they were needed. Men who owned 24 pubs and who could afford to get to matches in a private jet were carrying on like mad fellas who were still working for McAlpine and living in digs in Cricklewood. The rich Paddy is torn between his desire to flaunt it, and his equally strong desire to play the underdog, the outsider — even though he can pick up the phone and call a government minister at any time of the day or night and get things done, he has some emotional need to see himself still in the role of the rapparee, who acquired his wealth despite the best efforts of the Establishment to thwart him.

Though he must have quiet moments of truth when he realises that he, in fact, is now the Establishment, he feels that he functions much better as the wild man, the headcase.

It is another form of stage-Irishry, and it was played to the hilt during the Charlton years, just as it is played in the parade ring at Cheltenham when we see men who are worth a hundred million quid buck-lepping like labourers who have just won a lifetime's supply of free porter.

Jack's success was particularly potent for these boys, because of the patriotic dimension. Flying in your private plane to your executive box at a regular sporting event is deeply attractive, but if you're doing it for the love of your country, it is irresistible.

So, whether they liked it or not, Jack's lads were becoming part of the broader narrative of Irish success — in some versions, they were its founding fathers.

Official Ireland is fond of these simple generalisations, urging us to 'put on the green jersey', and even to 'give it a lash'. But as we have seen, a lot of other things were also happening in those years in Ireland, to change the way we were. It's just that football was the best thing, and it probably mattered the most. It was the best thing, and it didn't get any better than Italia 90.

Like the Summer of Love and punk rock, there is a time when the best energies seem to come together to create magic. And it can't last for very long, because it is too good, too intense. In fact, a lot of people are coming to it when it's already winding down, when it's over.

Jack would be the manager of the Republic of Ireland until the end of 1995, but it would dishonour the memories of Euro 88 and Italia 90 to say that it was still the same after that. There were wild nights, like the one in Windsor Park when we got the result to take us to America, surviving what had been a festival of hate. There were wonderful nights, most notably against Italy at the Giants Stadium in 1994. And yet when we think of that World Cup, we also think of the lads melting in the heat of Orlando, going out tamely to Holland and being dragged back to the Phoenix Park for an embarrassing homecoming.

We didn't even qualify for Euro 92, or Euro 96.

But the drinking didn't stop. The journey of Paul McGrath through these years reflects the way it was for a lot of us. His drinking was hardly even noticed during the glory days because when everyone is drunk, in the best possible way, no-one is drunk. Or at least they are feeling no pain. But that's not going to work forever. Alcoholism, they say, is a progressive illness, in the sense that it can only go one way — it can only get worse.

In the language of psycho-babble, Paul was 'enabled' to drink because he was our best player and we were getting so much out of him. And unusually for us, we didn't wait until he was dead for 20 years to realise how good he was, we knew it at the time. And we said it at the time.

It is now better understood that a person can be performing at a very high level and receiving all the affirmation that comes with that and still be in the throes of full-blown alcoholism — Tony Adams was the captain of Arsenal and England at the height of his addiction. And perhaps these things were not generally accepted in Paul's time, certainly not in football.

Back then, it was felt that the most compassionate thing you could do for a player with a drink problem was to keep it quiet. People were well-meaning, they just didn't know what they were doing. And there were times when it couldn't be kept quiet, like the day when Paul sat on the team bus outside Lansdowne Road for a match against Turkey and kept sitting when everyone else had left the bus. And kept sitting, unable to get off that bus.

Ah, the knees.

Not that we gentlemen of the press were on the path of enlightenment here either. We were no better than Corporate Paddy with his bullshit. We just wanted to make the party last.

But there comes a time when the party is over.

A lot of people, quite understandably, couldn't face life after it, and have been going around for the last fifteen years banging their bodhráns and playing the mad Paddy, the sort of people who'd be the first to shake the hand of Paul McGrath and buy him a drink.

If I knew then what I know now, I, too, would have realised back in 1990 that the party was over. And I'd have known exactly what was troubling Paul, because it was the same thing that was troubling myself. And I'd probably have written that autobiography with him, years before Vincent Hogan did it so well.

And Ireland would be free.

Ireland, in fact, was doing fine. And by the mid-90s, it was clear that another party was about to begin. But there was still a bit of fun to be had, out of the Charlton years.

In the last month of 1990, we elected our first woman President, Mary Robinson. Naturally, this turned into yet another battle in the ongoing civil war, which was now moving towards its decisive phase. Robinson was an iconic figure of the Left, one of the original feminists, a beautifully bred member of the liberal establishment and terrifyingly accomplished.

For sure, we could let her out in any company. There would be no hiding behind the couch when this lady appeared on *Newsnight*.

But when the campaign started, we were conditioned to assume that, as the Labour candidate, she was destined to finish third behind Austin Currie, representing Fine Gael, and Brian Lenihan, perhaps one of the few public figures in Ireland who could genuinely call himself a football man — he had played for UCD and Bohemians as a bustling centre-forward in the Noel Cantwell mould. But that would be no good to him when his campaign started unravelling, due to a few old porkies which were thrown back at him by the cold-blooded assassins of Dublin 4.

Perhaps it was just complacency, perhaps the tide really was going out on old Ireland, but from an apparently unassailable position, Lenihan suddenly started to look weak.

Though he had liberal credentials himself, due to his lifting of the censorship laws back in the day, in the mood of the time Robinson had all the momentum.

If there was any doubt that this was a continuation of the moral civil war, it all went away during a radio debate in which the Fianna Fáil contributor Pee Flynn couldn't stop himself making nasty remarks about Mrs Robinson suddenly discovering family values. There was probably nothing personal in it (or at least not much): it was just a bred-in-the-bone cultural response, a flashback to the days when Mary Robinson was one of the first people in Ireland to start openly using words like 'contraceptive pill', and perhaps even 'intrauterine device'.

Merely by saying such things she had made them a reality, in a place where, for all official purposes, they had not existed before.

And in the traditional version of family values which obtained at that time, if you were advancing the cause of women in areas such as the right to control their fertility, you were automatically damaging the concept of the family as it had been understood in Ireland since the time of Christ.

These were the family values that Pee Flynn pined for, and in his garbled way, he may have thought that reminding listeners of

Robinson's feminist record would damage her in the heartland. He didn't quite realise that a lot of voters might actually be ready to vote for such a woman, up against good ol' boys such as Lenihan and Currie, a woman whose brainy, lawyerly image had been softened by advisors such as Eoghan Harris.

And yet we tend to forget that Lenihan, after all the embarrassment, and the shafting by Haughey, and the fact that he didn't look a well man, still got the most votes. Again Paddy displayed the complex nature of his humanity here, voting for Lenihan in large numbers out of sympathy as much as anything else, and in appreciation of the fact that he had brought something to the party — but not voting for him in large enough numbers to stop Robinson winning the Presidency on Currie's transfers.

I voted for Robinson, predictably, because I knew which side I was on. Though over the years my view of her has darkened somewhat and not because she left for a really important role at the UN after her first term.

It's because I see her more clearly now as one of those patrician types who run everything, who just happens to be on the liberal wing, but who was born to rule regardless of her politics, the sort of people who don't have a job, they have a 'rôle'.

My own father had to leave secondary school at fourteen when his father died. He worked as a telegram boy while he studied for the Inter at night. Given that he eventually ended up at Inspector grade in the civil service, I have calculated that if he had started out where the Mary Robinsons of this world start out, he would quite comfortably have become Secretary General of the United Nations. And worked his way up from there.

Not that he ever displayed the slightest trace of bitterness about the cards that were dealt to him. Nor would it cross his mind that people like him kept football alive in this country, long before the Olé Olé's found their voice. But it would cross my mind from time to time.

And as for bringing me to see the then Boys In Green getting beaten in Dalymount Park, it didn't occur to him that he would live to see them playing in two out of the three World Cups for which they have qualified. He was just doing the fatherly thing, at the time, bringing me on the train to big football matches in the big city, filling my head with overpowering images which have never left me, taking home the match programme which I would re-read endlessly in bed at night, with the names of the players arranged according to their position on the park — Alan Kelly, Tony Dunne, Charlie Hurley, the great Giles.

Mary Robinson knew nothing of such things, I thought. Certainly I don't recall seeing her with all the folks up for the match in the Forte café beside Amiens Street station, eating bacon, eggs, beans and chips, tea, bread and butter, to set us up for a beating by Poland. In the mind's eye it is hard to see Mary Robinson watching us drawing with England on the big screen in the Submarine Bar in Crumlin, roaring obscenely at the referee to blow the whistle for full-time. Or driving drunk through the streets of Dublin after the draw with Holland, blowing her horn.

But she was still talking about the diaspora, about lighting a candle and putting it in the window of the Áras to show that we hadn't forgotten the emigrants. And in her own Harvard-educated way she seemed to know what she was talking about. She was talking about these things, about the children of the lost generations, around the time that Big Jack had Maurice Setters out looking for them. I guess it was just another of those happy accidents.

So whatever I think about her now, back then I was delighted to see her elected. At the end of this year of Italia 90 we were apparently still drunk enough on the fine wine of adventure to elect a liberal intellectual woman as head of state; in fact, we loved seeing her up there, a credit to us all. We had surprised ourselves again.

I remember running into Theo Dorgan on Grafton Street around that time, the two of us high on the improbability of it all. Neither of us could recall ever voting for anyone who had won anything and we were having some difficulty getting used to this new sensation, this growing belief that we had actually got it right for a change. During those days I would keep running into people I knew who seemed dazed with happiness, rolling back the years and savouring the strangeness of Mary Robinson becoming President of Ireland.

People were winning who had never won before.